D. EUGENE EGGER
THE PARADOX OF PLACE
IN THE LINE OF SIGHT

Publishers of Architecture, Art, and Design
Gordon Goff: Publisher

www.oroeditions.com
info@oroeditions.com

Published by ORO Editions

Copyright © Gregory A. Luhan, 2019
Text and Images © Gregory A. Luhan, 2019

All rights reserved. No part of this book may be reproduced, stored in a retrieval system, or transmitted in any form or by any means, including electronic, mechanical, photocopying of microfilming, recording, or otherwise (except that copying permitted by Sections 107 and 108 of the U.S. Copyright Law and except by reviewers for the public press) without written permission from the publisher.

You must not circulate this book in any other binding or cover and you must impose this same condition on any acquirer.

Editing and Design: Gregory A. Luhan
Project Coordinator: Kirby Anderson

10 9 8 7 6 5 4 3 2 1 First Edition

Library of Congress data available upon request. World Rights: Available

ISBN: 978-1-941806-31-9

Color Separations and Printing: ORO Group Ltd.
Printed in China.

International Distribution: www.oroeditions.com/distribution

ORO Editions makes a continuous effort to minimize the overall carbon footprint of its publications. As part of this goal, ORO Editions, in association with Global ReLeaf, arranges to plant trees to replace those used in the manufacturing of the paper produced for its books. Global ReLeaf is an international campaign run by American Forests, one of the world's oldest nonprofit conservation organizations. Global ReLeaf is American Forests' education and action program that helps individuals, organizations, agencies, and corporations improve the local and global environment by planting and caring for trees.

D. EUGENE EGGER
THE PARADOX OF PLACE
IN THE LINE OF SIGHT

Edited, *Gregory A. Luhan, Ph.D.*

Foreword, *Kenneth Frampton*
Afterword, *Frank H. Weiner*

Contributors
Richard Blythe
Steven House
Cathi House
Mitzi Vernon
Paul Emmons
Mark A. Blizard
Michael OBrien
Gregory A. Luhan

CONTENTS

Introduction
Richard Blythe
6

Foreword – Simultaneity & Experience: The Drawings of Gene Egger
Kenneth Frampton
8

Acknowledgments
10

Means of Design Learning
Dayton Eugene Egger
14

Study Abroad: The Educational Legacy at Virginia Tech
Dayton Eugene Egger
16

Travel Sketches — Europe
20

Learning to See
Steven + Cathi House (House + House Architects)
144

Storytelling, The Lines of Gene Egger
Mitzi Vernon
148

Never a Day Without a Line: Traveling Sketchbooks and Education of Architects
Paul Emmons
152

Field Studies
Mark Blizard
156

Learning by Observing
Michael OBrien
162

Travel Sketches — North America
164

Timelessness and Currency: Drawing as an Embodied Signature
Gregory A. Luhan
200

Travel Sketches — Europe Programs, 1969-2018
208

Afterword – The Pedagogy of the Sketch
Frank H. Weiner
232

Contributors
236

INTRODUCTION

Richard Blythe

On a December morning in the early 1990s I walked into the Il Campo Siena, sketchbook in one hand and partner in the other. She sought out a sunny segment in which to read while I began to explore. We were each in our way taking in the place. As I paced, notated, and sketched I became aware, above the general din of a town waking up, of a disturbance. An irritated woman fist-waving and yelling from a populated table on the far side. I stole a conspiratorial look at my partner to see if she had noticed. She had abandoned her book, was laughing and glancing tangentially from me to the shouting woman. The woman leaned forward from behind a long table set with cloth and metal chairs standing on the high edge of Il Campo in the sun. The faces of those seated either side looked toward her and she directly at me. I was the cause of the disturbance and object of derision. I have remained curious ever since to understand better my offense.

Egger's drawings, monstrous X-rays as they are, are powerful posing two kinds of danger to the place from which each takes and as such offers a clue to my dilemma. There is something about making a drawing, some prosthetic advantage, a sort of telescope through which new worlds appear through the application of precise labours producing an extraction out of the very fabric that precedes the contact of pen tip and paper, something beyond what the eye casually sees.

Drawing is revealing and perhaps in the case of my antagonist, distressingly so – she did not like the feel of my glasses upon her place knowing that I was taking something of it, touching it with my eye and pen. She also knew that there was more than just a theft in action, that indeed in making the drawing and "taking in" this place I was also making something, a new version of the Il Campo itself that was mine. Drawings are projective as the essays in this book attest.

New kinds of possibilities occupy the interstices of drawing and world. The following essays explain how Egger understood the power of revealing this grimoire (to borrow from Marco Frascari, another of Virginia Tech's proponents of the architectural drawing) to the more than 1500 students who travelled with him over the years. Moreover,

INTRODUCTION

from which might flow their monstrous combinations of measure and plan and section and view and register as "experiences" for the subsequent millions that would inhabit that architecture. Perhaps these inhabitants, in turn, would come to love their monsters, would rise even to fist-waving and yelling. Beware of drawings. They show us things unseeable, they change us, and by the time you have seen one, it is too late to turn back.

Egger's "Pocahontas: View from Supervisor House" is an essay in its own right on the displacements and separations at play between a town and its overseer captured in a single image. In a millisecond we have lived the walk on the path, the stairs, felt the vertigo of the conversations and heard the gossip through the inversion of the house rendered upside down in the lower hemisphere of the drawing. Through our reading, we have lived the agonies and the sadness, the joys and friendships that play out between a town and its supervisor. Poetics does this, rendering a specific scene at one particular point in time with an idiosyncratic hand but it does so in such a way that the scene takes shape within us, the reader as if it were our unique moment. This publication is a book of poetic drawings, a grimoire, and full of elegant dangers and monsters.

This book captures a critical part of the history of Virginia Tech and of the foundational myth of drawing that resonates still today in studios and field trips. This book collects together evidence of Egger's practice of drawing, one that is both architectural and educational. This evidence demonstrates the efficacy of such practices and methods in the production of disciplinary knowledge. Exploratory or, if you like, venturous practices like the drawing practice of Egger, will guide the College of Architecture and Urban Studies in realizing the Virginia Tech Beyond Boundaries vision.

FOREWORD
Simultaneity & Experience: The Drawings of Gene Egger

Kenneth Frampton

> *The monuments of Europe are being worn out by Kodaks.*
> *Anonymous*
> *Circa 1950*

It is safe to say that today in our architectural schools nobody draws anymore and that digital technology is now so advanced that one is hard-pressed to get even a thumbnail sketch out of the average student of architecture. The computer, the cell phone, and the internet carry everything before them and with this onslaught perception itself is subtly transformed in ways that we don't fully understand. Thus, it is possible for students today to dismiss most drawings as anachronistic exercises; however, these interpretations would be fallacious.

The drawings of Dayton Eugene (Gene) Egger represent the simultaneity of experience as a device for creative empowerment – particularly at those moments when the artist sets us before the interstitial labyrinth of the traditional European city which today we are barely able to perceive, let alone represent or maintain. These are travel sketches which continually trace the displacement of the human subject in space. As in the case of Egger's x-ray renderings of Le Corbusier's Ronchamp Chapel going so far as to attempt an existential dissolution of its space as this may be experienced in time, both within and without, thereby simulating the trope of a doubly exposed negative which digital photography no longer permits. At times the draughtsman's acute observation of detail draws our attention away from the displacement of space to focus on incidental detail, such as the syncopated patterning of a piece of tilework. This intentional distraction inescapably evokes the flow of time via a constant allusion to ruination either real or imagined.

Egger's cut-away perspective provokes the imagination through fictions as if a seismic event that, had it taken place, would have engulfed the artist himself. The shaky ink line, evidently a signature, serves as an aide memoire, through which the author retains the experiential moment of a particularly moving spatial episode. In this regard, Egger's sketches inextricably depict places as a series of dimensional complexities from vantage points that suggest a three-way spatial displacement wherein one has either to pass up or down via adjacent staircases in the foreground or, alternatively, forge ahead on axis to penetrate the perspective in depth. These tonalities are an integral part of Egger's pedagogical motivations.

Egger's gossamer traces of fine ink encompass the viewer, their outlines delineating a seemingly large, calm and ample space that the artist has just exited to enter into the labyrinthine prospect of some concatenated Piranesian space. Such strategic moments often set before a channel of space between the flanking walls of adjacent houses looking down over a great distance, as Schinkel might have done, onto the distant expanse of an Italian hill town shrouded in the heat haze of high summer. At other times, one passes through the sketches, as though a flâneur wandering through a collection of alternative stage sets, while on other occasions the vision veers towards the cinematic and, with this, one eventually arrives in Venice.

Except for the detailed examination of modern European architecture by Le Corbusier, Carlo Scarpa, and Luigi Snozzi and the American rural hamlets of Virginia and West Virginia, Egger's Cubist-inspired drawings are exclusively pre-occupied with Europe, primarily Italy. His images seem to cut through Europe's medieval fabric to simultaneously reveal detail and spatial configuration – in particular those spaces inspired by the Italian Renaissance. Caught between the lost ethos of the grand tour and the admass accessibility of contemporary tourism, Egger's obsessive vision skillfully superimposes arcades and galleria while offering the occasional relief afforded by a passing Purist glimpse of a café terrace. His drawing technique enables the viewer to enter the sublime vaults of Giuseppe Mazzoni's Galleria Vittorio Emanuelle, only to search in vain for the Italian Stile Floreale and to find nothing of the exotic fin de siècle Milanese figures as Raimondo D'Aronco or Giuseppe Sommaruga.

Egger's drawings suspend us in a particular moment of time, where his emphatically modernist vision tactically skirts and skims the architectural modernity that was once such an intrinsic part of design education. These drawings are to be valued as an American academic architectural vision quite literally drawn from a particular moment in time contemporaneously looking both backward to the past and forward through both time and space, toward a possible future.

ACKNOWLEDGMENTS

I EXPRESS MY SINCERE GRATITUDE TO ALL OF MY COLLEAGUES – friends, faculty mentors, and fellow architects who contributed their time, drawings, and stories to help make this book project a reality. This project demonstrates the professional respect that we share individually and collectively for Dayton Eugene Egger. As educators, researchers, thought leaders, and friends, we saw inestimable value in unearthing the extensive collection of pedagogical sketches, that until 2016, were never seen in their entirety. We believe that this amassed collection, which initially served as an invaluable guide for thousands of students who traveled and studied with Gene in Virginia Tech's study abroad programs, could extend beyond initial experience to deepen and inform architectural education. The impetus for this publication originated in the knowledge of the magnitude of Egger's drawings accumulated over a nearly five-decade educational career. This awareness informed conversations with Dean Mitzi Vernon of the University of Kentucky College of Design, who had the opportunity to travel with Gene while she was a graduate student at Virginia Tech in the mid-1990s. Together, we invited Gene – along with his wife Dorothy and daughter Kirsten – to Lexington to present his drawings to audiences that extend well beyond Blacksburg. From January to August of 2016, my students Thomas Lanham, Oliver Hidalgo, Andrew Meyer, Terrence Dankwa, and I scanned and digitally corrected each drawing and then printed them on Fabriano paper for the exhibition. The team partnered with Gerald Hovermale of Lexington's Picture Perfect Custom Framing for matting and framing. We also worked with the College's Lectures + Exhibition Committee and Celeste Lewis, Director of the Pam Miller Downtown Arts Center, to secure a space for the exhibition and an associated public lecture, which coincided with Lexington's September Gallery Hop. Over 500 people attended the event demonstrating the value and impact that the drawn line has on the community at-large.

During Gene's trip to Lexington, we arranged for him to meet with students enrolled in our design foundations program. These same students participated in a two-day immersive drawing experience in historic downtown Midway and at the Wild Turkey Distillery in Lawrenceburg, Kentucky. I wish to extend my gratitude to Charlotte Leedy,

Sabrina Brewer, Kimberly Light, Ginny Miller, Julie Wilson, Lori Matthews, and Margaret Grizzle for assisting with the seamless completion of the exhibition, lecture, interviews, and filmography. I also thank Adam Wiseman of PrintLex for his generosity in providing the vinyl banners for the exhibit and Allison May for photographing the exhibition and field study in Midway, Kentucky. I am grateful to April Pottorff, FAIA for hosting the post-lecture dinner and Richard Levine for showcasing his house at Raven Run as part of the festivities. I offer special thanks to my fall 2016 third-year design studio: Terrence Dankwa, Nicole Felicetti, Cameron Ginter, Karalynn Graves, Blane Hornung, Freddy Maggiorani, Sydnee Rigsby, Mary Katherine Schaefer, Taylor Stephens, Trevor Tanzi, William Tingle, Vanessa Vidal Ladera, Shengmian Wang, and Vincent West, who helped develop and set up the *Places of Place* exhibition.

The book comprises three parts – Gene Egger's pedagogy as sparked by travels to Europe and North America and its direct impact on students as evidenced through drawing. Essay contributions by Kenneth Frampton, Dayton Eugene Egger, Steven + Cathi House, Mitzi Vernon, Paul Emmons, Mark Blizard, Michael OBrien, Gregory Luhan, and Frank Weiner bridge these three "chapters" and provide critical insights or personal reflections. Kenneth Frampton's Foreword characterizes Gene Egger's sketches as images that capture the simultaneity of experience and representation. Frampton describes the graphic content of these images as spatial episodes that visually depict a given place from multiple vantage points. To Frampton, these "concatenated Piranesian spaces" are invaluable to the American academic architectural vision. Further, the method used by Professor Egger is an essential device for students, faculty, and architects to understand and convey both place and space at moments in time. Dayton Eugene Egger's "Means of Design Learning" states his pedagogical agenda and offers insights into the precise and reciprocal engagement between the faculty and students. To Egger, architectural education is a vibrant vehicle for creating and disseminating knowledge across generations. It simultaneously concerns learning from the past and presents possible futures. Egger points to lessons learned from Josef Albers related to the "criticality of seeing" and displaying information. To Egger, these discursive departure points engage both the place of potential discovery and the act of applying knowledge to a given situation and a given context. Egger's "Study Abroad: The Educational Legacy at Virginia Tech" describes the Virginia Tech Study Abroad experience as an essential element of the College of Architecture and Urban Studies pedagogical processes. Egger states that by bringing students from Virginia to the world narrows the gap between the textbook and the classroom. Egger further describes the experience as an extension of the academic environment that enables deeper learning through sensorial experience, rational objectification, and constructive synthesis. The drawings and notations produced during these experiences not only capture the appearance and significance of a place but also convey its presence over time and offers insights into its reinvention.

Steven + Cathi House's "Learning to See" examines Gene Egger's five-decades-long dedication to the architectural education as an extended poetic expression that instills, inspires, and captures moments of "spontaneous awareness." The Houses compare and contrast a variety of media to convey visual phenomena and use Egger's travel sketches as a vibrant sounding board to reflect on the parallel complexities often confronted in the built environment. The Houses further describe Egger's sketches as editing devices capable of "stripping away extraneous details" to enable the viewer to see firsthand the spirit of the building or a place. Mitzi Vernon's "Storytelling: The Lines of Gene Egger" recounts her traveling experiences with Gene Egger as compositional short stories across all scales. Vernon describes drawing as a transparent layering process that moves through space and records the encounter with a particular place. Vernon extols Egger's innate ability to use the architectural sketch as an explanatory device that elicits the essence of a place in a way that a photograph or written text could not possibly capture. She notes that, through drawing, Egger constructs and conveys the building, the town square, or the village through compositional strategies that also suggest additional complexity by revealing a context through details. Paul Emmons's "Never a Day without a Line: Traveling Sketchbooks and Education of Architects" presents the nature of traveling and the necessity of visually documenting the travel experience as essential requirements of architectural education. Emmons describes visual travel journals as the "accumulation of drawing skills" that inform and educate future generations of architects. Emmons invokes the travelogues of the Grand Tour to cast the immediacy of artistic creation as a tool for discovery. Mark Blizard's "Field Studies" discusses the design laboratory taught by Professor Gene Egger as a timeless and perpetually relevant space of discovery and exchange. The context of the sketchbook and its subsequent translation into field studies demarcate radical sites for architectural inquiry. In this sense, the sketchbook is a journalistic device that capably reveals visual phenomena, complexity, and accumulated history. The sketch, in turn, enables the author and reader/viewer to see beneath surfaces through layered transparency, multiple points of views, and inscribed narratives. Together the drawing and sketchbook initiate a formative dialogue between place and artist that expresses both the visible and invisible contours of a given site. Michael OBrien's "Learning by Observing" appends an outsider's perspective to Gene Egger's pedagogical scaffolding, the rigor of his study abroad experiences, the spatial underpinnings of his thinking, and the formal logics that facilitated discovery for generations of architecture students. OBrien's essay proposes a "structured listening" through which a sequence of drawings and annotations convey proportions, principles, and other acquired and synthesized knowledge that informs architecture. Gregory Luhan's "Timelessness and Currency: Drawing as an Embodied Signature" enlists conversations with Antoine Predock to develop three lenses through which to understand Gene Egger's pedagogical travel sketches as being both timeless and emphatically of the moment. The three themes relate to the architect's inner impulse, the revelation of place, and the embodied signature. Each topic organically connects the act of drawing to the traditional registers of architecture and demonstrates how the gestural lines liberate the presentation while revealing the hidden truths of place. Luhan describes Egger's drawings as a flexible framework for examining site through the "thin film of cultural intervention" in which the architect and student graphically present the past, present, and prospects of a setting with particular emphasis on the regional examination of several Appalachian mining towns. Frank Weiner's afterword, entitled "The Pedagogy of the Sketch," opens a new door to the sketches to advocate for releasing Egger's sketches from historical accuracy or necessitating that the viewer comparatively examines hundreds of historical sketches against photographs of a place. For Weiner, Egger's sketches are primarily pedagogical tools that peel away the layers of a context to reveal both the author's intention and the place's meaning. The tonality of Weiner's contribution encompasses Egger's study abroad as well as his visit to Lexington.

    This acknowledgment would not be complete without recognizing the support of Dean Richard Blythe of Virginia Tech, who contributed an invaluable introduction to the book project and provided the subvention to enable its production. I recognize Stephen Caffey for his editorial and scholarly contribution, Faith Harders for her curatorial insights, Heinrich Schnoedt for assisting with the study abroad image identification, and Gordon Goff of ORO Editions for seeing the value of Gene's work and for enabling the national and international distribution of this publication. Ultimately, to Gene, thank you for challenging all of us to see and experience the world and to represent it in a way that is timelessly meaningful and perpetually impactful.

MEANS OF DESIGN LEARNING
Comments On Teaching

Dayton Eugene Egger

It should be the chief aim of a university professor to exhibit himself in his own true character – that is, as an ignorant man thinking, actively utilizing his small share of knowledge.[1]
Alfred North Whitehead, The Aims of Education

Teaching is reciprocally tied to the continued learning of the teacher. While I believe that my way of working can contribute to effective learning in any discipline, I am restricting my thoughts here to the Teaching/Learning strategies necessary in a professional Architecture + Design Curriculum.

Good teaching is simply the ability to create and maintain a rhythmic learning environment that crafts cycles of independence and discipline between our daily concerns, abilities, and conflicts (independence) and the precise knowledge (discipline) demanded by our subject of study. What we bring to a learning experience contains legitimate personal abilities that have already been effective in developing our intellectual and sensible growth. We must, for example, bring a critical examination of our personal history as a tool to know how to see what is right in front of us in unfamiliar situations. Or as our best poets understand, "seeing the familiar in the strange" and the reverse, "seeing the strange in the familiar.[2]"

I have found that the productive study of any subject is to rescue it from the numbing effect of familiarity. Josef Albers' example of "critical seeing" is demonstrated when: holding up three fingers, he asks how many is this? His answer is not three but five by counting the fingers and the spaces between and therefore the more complete phenomena or as he calls it the psychological effect of knowing; or as A. N. Whitehead distinguishes "factual realities from actual realities.[3]"

Learning is not always an acquisition of something new but is more likely to be a new configuration of something that we may already possess. It is the building of tools to open a situation, exposing the ordered patterns of its important elements and thereby its legible structure. Building an active dialogue between the NOMINAL existence of an event and the PHENOMENAL presence of the event's character is essential to learning or acquiring the critical knowledge necessary for making clear, habitable places.

The popular chronicle *Seeing is Forgetting the Name of the Thing One Sees* replays Robert Irwin's emerging dependence in painting on his responding directly to the quality of each situation that he created. Rejecting the a priori images that interfered with his perception of the actual nature of the immediate moment Irwin has elevated "situational thinking" as the important perceptual means to recognize fundamental forces that shape our environmental perceptual experience. Lindon Leader's FedEx logo, with the subliminal arrow, is an excellent example of a double meaning created by letters and the collateral space of the specially crafted font. Using the complementary opposites blue/violet and red/orange the logo automatically takes on a "double" sense of dynamic movement.

Specifically, traditional nominal references that imply the meaning of a built environment, such as "living room" or "bathroom" do not tell about how its making or how it addresses its materiality. On the surface, reading the patterns of movement controls the placement of objects, the light that focuses different areas calculates the spatial qualities, the materials that reflect or absorb light/shadow or sound sustains a haptic necessity of habitation. These dimensions speak to immediate, descriptive dialog, but they are also dependent on the order and means of making the room. What movement, light and material share are the order of the place, both physical and categorical or the "how" determines the "what."

Grasping and understanding the "how" in our decisions when designing things or situations is also to confront the great history of ideas in our profession of architecture. It is to grapple, in a heuristic, iterative process that takes intense, productive thought/time to uncover, in ill-defined problem environments, the critical forces at play in any product realization. It is to think of the means with which we build not only to believe in the conventional or nominal representations of elemental parts of a whole.

Ideas in architecture are spatial, physical and cultural thoughts invested with how. In effect, they are ideas that combine otherwise separate entities. Realizing one's ideas in form is an essential ability gained in early design education. Being able actually to do what you intend architecturally takes one beyond the conventional naming of the parts assemblage and intended purpose and is, from my point of view, the most difficult ability to acquire.

NOTES

[1] Whitehead, A. N. (1959). *The Aims of Education*. Daedalus, 88(1), pp. 192-205.
[2] Populous technique for creative thought, originally credited as an 18th Century German origin, is also seen in the Romanticists English poets, Wordsworth and Coleridge.
[3] Whitehead, A. N. (1929). *Process and Reality*. New York: Macmillan, p. 86.

STUDY ABROAD
The Educational Legacy at Virginia Tech

Dayton Eugene Egger

Living among vast human accomplishments defines the luxury of our modern community and prepares us to contribute to this great treasure – or, at least, not to damage it should be the goal of design education. Studying this built environment and the processes for building it poses the difficult task of learning more about what we assume we already know. What we bring to situations, the presentative artifacts, and relevant cultural and historical containers play crucial roles in the pedagogical process. Confronting these vast treasures also challenges our attempts to order, to understand, and to come to terms with the brevity of the encounter – brief not only because of limited time but because of our limited means to sustain inquiry. Human experience can go beyond the memory or record of an event. Jerome Brunner reminds us that "Learning should not only take us somewhere; it should allow us later to go further more easily."[1] We come to realize that a significant learning experience extends our ability to recreate that experience apart from the original circumstances that created it.

Learning, as well as subjects to be learned, deserves autonomy. Fundamental similarities among apparently dissimilar subjects are grasped, if not immediately controlled, by the alert learner. Changing the scale of city readings, for example, such as seeing streets as rooms, building facades as room walls, and urban monuments as precious belongings within the room present a lasting perceptual ordering in space. To understand, for example, that the fundamental operational order behind Aldo Rossi's contemporary Cemetery of San Cataldo is the same as the adjacent nineteenth-century cemetery by Andrea Costa frees form from simplistic functional determinacy. Design "connectedness" sharpens design's instrumental device and enhances it as a vehicle to remember and understand more deeply our encounter.

The Means of Design Learning

When teaching drawing from nature, Johannes Itten gave his design students a sequential assignment: "Interpret the object first expressively, then constructively, then naturalistically and finally in a valid design synthesis."[2] Itten's 1919 Vorkurs (Basic Course) at the Weimar Bauhaus aimed to free students gradually "from dead conventions and to take courage for the work of their own." Teaching the "means of design" meant that the students had to become receptive to their individuality, temperament, and talents. "This alone makes for a creative atmosphere that encourages original work," Itten said. "The work should be genuine. The student should gain natural self-confidence and eventually find his profession."

Maintaining an authentic creative learning environment and learning through play and personal speculation was a common principle in Itten's Basic Course, reflecting nineteenth-century learning strategies pioneered by Friedrich Fröbel, Johann Pestalozzi, and Maria Montessori. The developmental, subjective nature of learning paralleled introductions of objective concepts, fact, and technology. Itten cycled his students through the three-step learning process of initiating a vivid visual experience, followed by intellectual explanation, concluding with the execution of the design task at hand. Analysis does not automatically precede action. Each step is concertedly active.

The Significance of Study Abroad

Nurturing student ability to study the wholeness of cultural artifacts and the formative artistic forces with which each lives is the goal of our study abroad program. We endeavor to study our architectural, urban encounters in three ways: to sensibly experience, to objectify rationally, and to realize as a synthesis. Each means confronts the individuality of the student as well as the permanency of the artifact. Simultaneously sustaining immediate subjective experience with extended objective recognition borrows from Gadamer's assertion that we transform in the process of encountering the work of art.[3]

On our contemporary heuristic, developmental, and experiential processes of grasping and using knowledge highlights, for example, Le Corbusier's comments: "When one travels and works with visual things – architecture, painting or sculpture – one uses one's eyes and draws, to fix deep down in one's experience what is seen . . . To Draw oneself to trace the lines, handle the volumes, organize the surface . . . Once the pencil has recorded the impression, it stays for good, entered, registered, inscribed . . . all this means first to look, and then to observe, and finally perhaps to discover . . ."[4]

Dayton Eugene Egger

Encounters, Readings, and Gestures

OUR ABILITIES TO GENUINELY FEEL, SEE, AND THINK MUST REFERENCE BOTH HISTORICAL RELATEDNESS AND PURPOSE. These abilities heighten our kinship to the places we inhabit even as visitors. A direct encounter with our built heritage implies the necessity of travel and is a primary way to shape our knowledge and readiness to learn. Architecture known only by its names and uses denies the continuous development of the human experience that it forges. Only the poverty of our imagination reduces an encounter with art to the artists' intention or the artifacts' utility. Encounters with architectural form should not stop at its power as a signifier of function, culture, power, or other "meaning" inferred by the viewer. The built environment embodies a visual "language" as valid as other forms of communication. Our obligation is to learn some form of this "language" since we occupy the built environment all of our lives.

How a thing "appears" and how it "is," a question that historically occupied philosophical debate is crucial in contemporary design discourse. The structural-functional dialogue toward form and the sign-symbol extension toward meaning do not replace the built referent but increase the dimensions of knowing it, of conceiving organizing ideas with it. The continuing, changing presence and experience of the artifact is the co-reality of our studies as we visit places in our travels that are imbued with learned as well as discoverable significance.

Living and studying in a foreign setting focuses attention on issues more likely taken for granted in familiar surroundings. For the environmental designer, rescuing a subject of study from the numbing effect of familiarity is an important step in the acquisition of new knowledge. Wittgenstein notes, "The aspects of things that are most important for us are hidden because of their simplicity and familiarity."[5] Being able to "see" solutions, forms and processes within the aesthetic, environmental configurations around us is a prerequisite to effective reading and understanding.

While inextricably bound to sky, horizon, and earth, architecture has remarkably few primary compositional elements. Kandinsky's analysis of pictorial elements, point, and line to (picture) plane, reminds us of a deeply rooted simplicity of form. "Point – repose. Line – inner tension, derived from motion. Both elements – intersections, juxtapositions that create their language, unattainable in words. Cutting out the frills, which muffle and obscure the inner sound of this language, gives pictorial expression the utmost conciseness and the utmost precision. The pure form offers its services to living content." Steven Holl gently returns us to the "proto-elements" in an architecture of LINES, PLANES, AND VOLUMES. The means of architectural composition, their colors and deformations in specific situations, activate a means to read Architecture and also to "recite" these readings.[6]

Elements of architecture, embellished or pure, are an open-ended means of endorsing, framing, and signifying content. As Jerome Brunner would say, the possibility orders them in a way that permits extrapolation or interpolation or conversion into another form.[7] In turn, recognition of significance does not exclude the vehicle that carries it. Not reduced to utility nor romanticized to ruins, the inhabitable form may be experienced and significantly re-lived at different times and circumstances.

Built form, buildings as landscape, seen together at small or large scale, should be gathered, studied, and re-invented. Our drawings and notations always strive to show the fullness of form, (unseen geometry and tectonic necessity) with its appearance (bound identity, setting, and material) and its public presence, (the splendor of a coherent whole) to be experienced over time. The narrative may emerge, or it may initiate, but it seldom determines.

NOTES

[1] Bruner, J. S. (1977). *The Process of Education*, Cambridge, MA: Harvard University Press, p. 17.
[2] Itten, J. (1975). *Design and Form: The Basic Course at the Bauhaus*, English Translation, John Wiley & Sons, Inc. and Thames and Hudson Ltd., London, p. 74.
[3] Gadamer, H. G. (1975). *Truth and Method*. New York: Seabury Press, p. 36.
[4] Le Corbusier, (1960). *Creation Is a Patient Search*. New York: Praeger, p. 63.
[5] Wittgenstein, L. (1958). *Philosophical Investigations*. Third Edition, trans. G.E.M. Anscombe. New York: Basil Blackwell & Mott, Ltd., p. 50e, section 129.
[6] Holl, S. (1996). *Anchoring*, New York: Princeton Architectural Press, p. 26.
[7] Bruner, J. S. (1966). *Toward a Theory of Instruction*. Cambridge, MA: Harvard University Press, pp. 49–53.

20

EUROPE

EUROPE

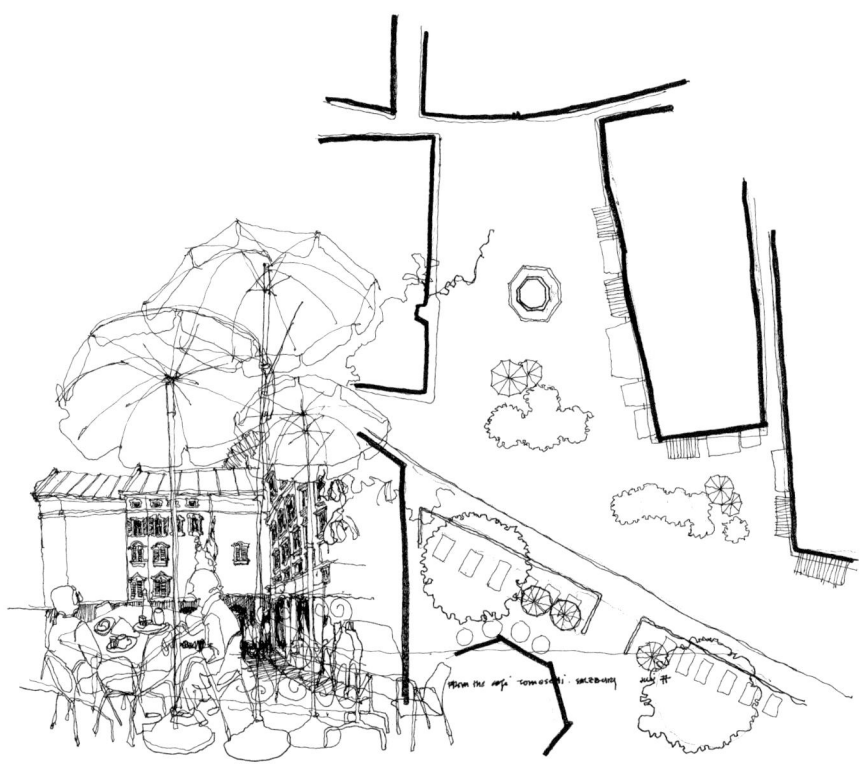

CAFE TOMASELLI - 01
Austria, Salzburg (July 1977)
Pen and Ink Drawing on Fabriano Paper
33.02 cm x 48.26 cm (13 in x 19 in)

THE PARADOX OF PLACE: IN THE LINE OF SIGHT

ALTER MARKET - SALZBURG ET TOMASELLI
Austria, Salzburg (25 August 1974)
Pen and Ink Drawing on Fabriano Paper
33.02 cm x 48.26 cm (13 in x 19 in)

EUROPE

 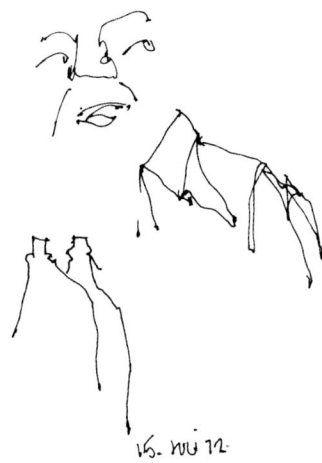

SCHLOSSWIRT ZUANIFT BARTMIXER
Austria, Salzburg (15 July 1972)
Pen and Ink Drawing on Fabriano Paper
33.02 cm x 48.26 cm (13 in x 19 in)

THE PARADOX OF PLACE: IN THE LINE OF SIGHT

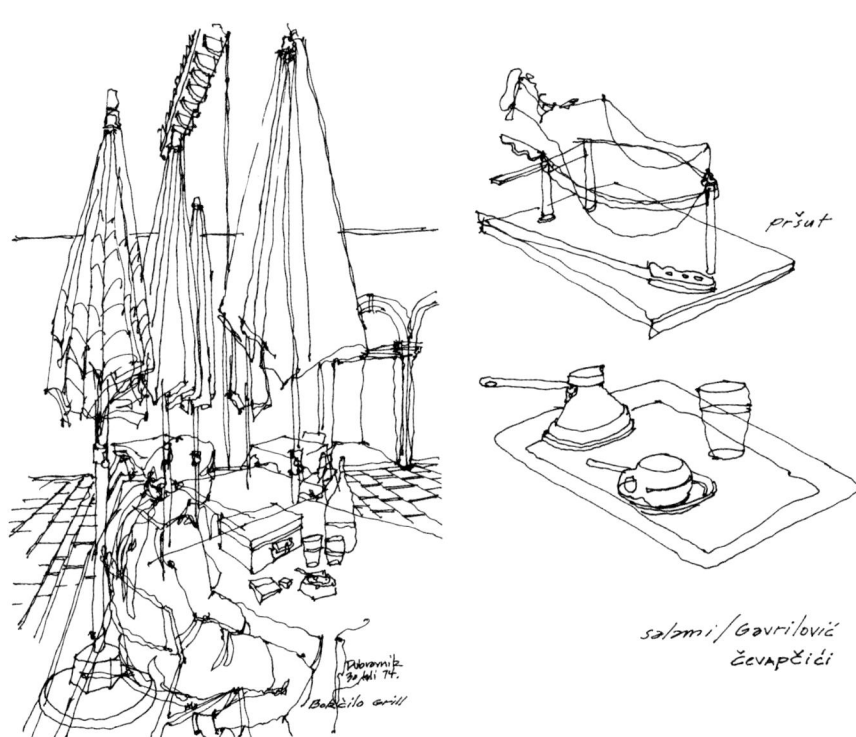

TURKISH COFFEE / SALAMI / GAVRILOVIC CEVAPCICI
Croatia, Dubrovnik (30 July 1974)
Pen and Ink Drawing on Fabriano Paper
33.02 cm x 48.26 cm (13 in x 19 in)

EUROPE

DUBROVNIK - 01
Croatia, Dubrovnik (30 July 1974)
Pen and Ink Drawing on Fabriano Paper
33.02 cm x 48.26 cm (13 in x 19 in)

THE PARADOX OF PLACE: IN THE LINE OF SIGHT

DUBROVNIK - 02
Croatia, Dubrovnik (30 July 1974)
Pen and Ink Drawing on Fabriano Paper
33.02 cm x 48.26 cm (13 in x 19 in)

EUROPE

DOLE - 01
France, Dole (23 June 2002)
Pen and Ink Drawing on Fabriano Paper
33.02 cm x 48.26 cm (13 in x 19 in)

THE PARADOX OF PLACE: IN THE LINE OF SIGHT

SAINTE MARIE DE LA TOURETTE - DORMITORY CORRIDOR
France, Eveux (10 June 1992)
Pen and Ink Drawing on Fabriano Paper
33.02 cm x 48.26 cm (13 in x 19 in)

EUROPE

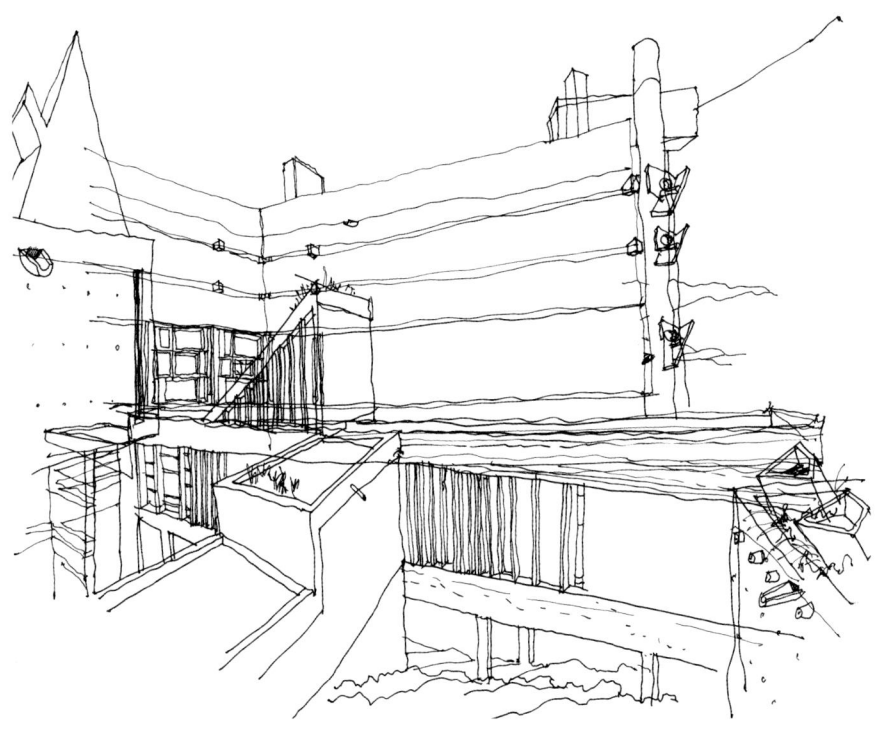

SAINTE MARIE DE LA TOURETTE - INTERIOR COURTYARD
France, Eveux (10 June 1992)
Pen and Ink Drawing on Fabriano Paper
33.02 cm x 48.26 cm (13 in x 19 in)

THE PARADOX OF PLACE: IN THE LINE OF SIGHT

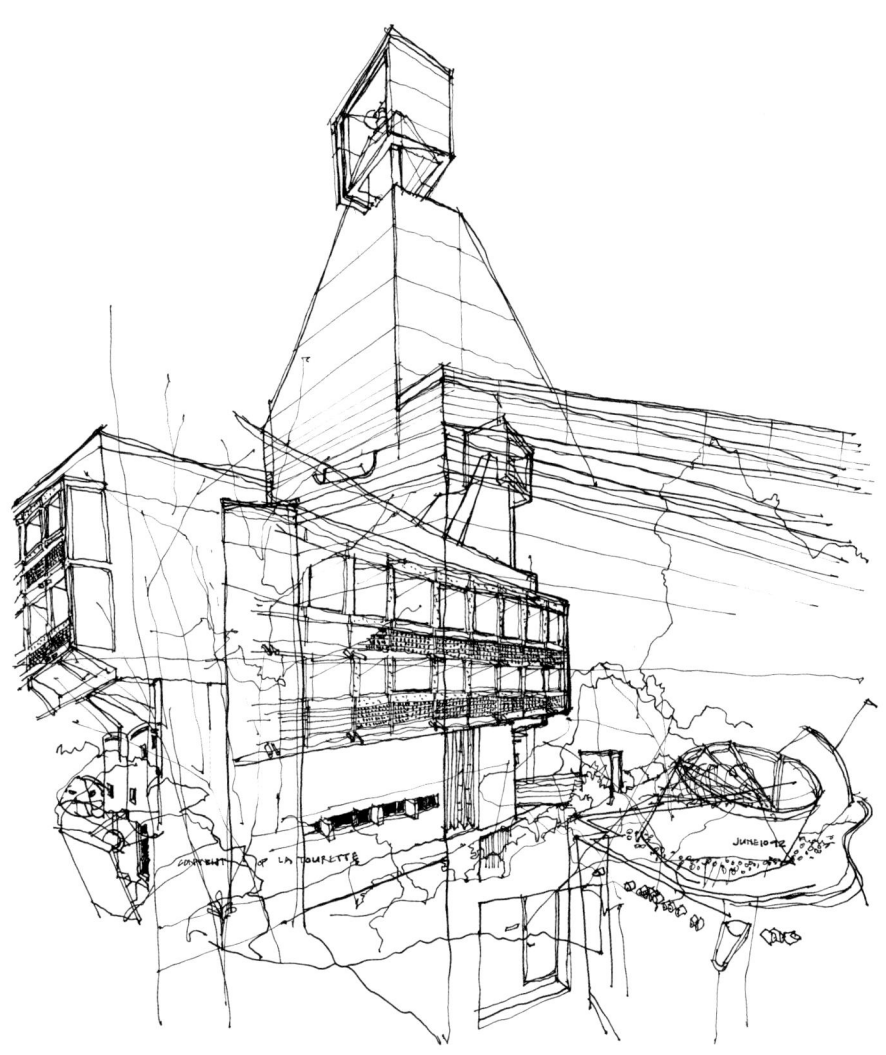

SAINTE MARIE DE LA TOURETTE - COMPOSITION OF LA TOURETTE
France, Eveux (10 June 1992)
Pen and Ink Drawing on Fabriano Paper
33.02 cm x 48.26 cm (13 in x 19 in)

EUROPE

LE THORONET ABBEY - CLOISTER
France, Le Thoronet (Undated)
Pen and Ink Drawing on Fabriano Paper
33.02 cm x 48.26 cm (13 in x 19 in)

THE PARADOX OF PLACE: IN THE LINE OF SIGHT

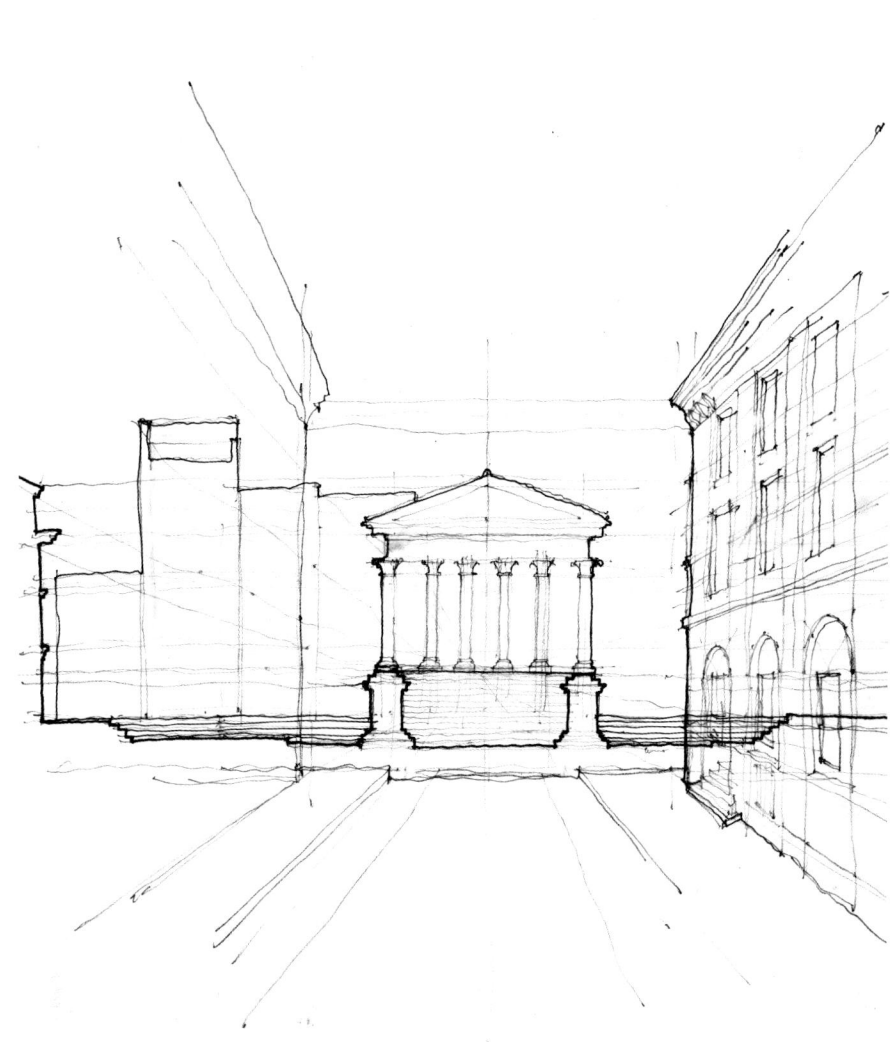

MAISON CARRE
France, Nimes (Undated)
Pen and Ink Drawing with Pencil on Fabriano Paper
33.02 cm x 48.26 cm (13 in x 19 in)

EUROPE

VILLA SAVOYE - BATH
France, Poissy (Undated)
Pen and Ink Drawing on Fabriano Paper
33.02 cm x 48.26 cm (13 in x 19 in)

THE PARADOX OF PLACE: IN THE LINE OF SIGHT

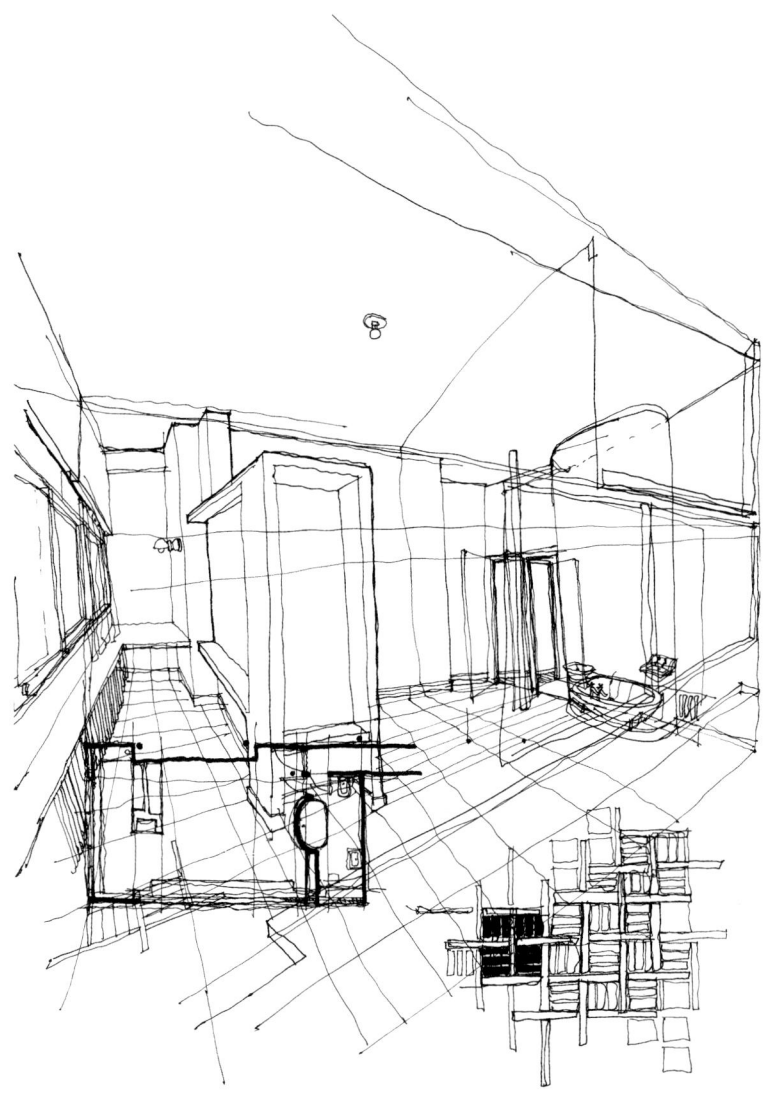

VILLA SAVOYE - BEDROOM
France, Poissy (Undated)
Pen and Ink Drawing on Fabriano Paper
33.02 cm x 48.26 cm (13 in x 19 in)

EUROPE

NOTRE DAME DU HAUT - MORPHOLOGY DU PLAN
France, Ronchamp (07 June 1992)
Pen and Ink Drawing on Fabriano Paper
33.02 cm x 48.26 cm (13 in x 19 in)

THE PARADOX OF PLACE: IN THE LINE OF SIGHT

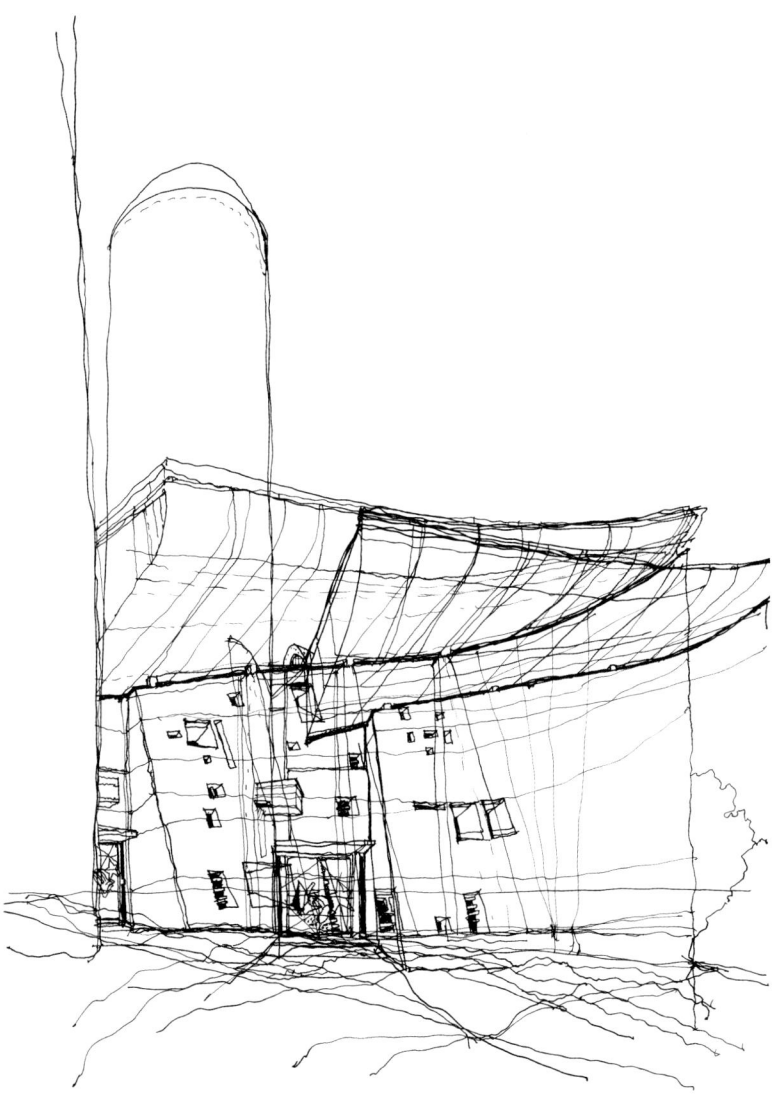

NOTRE DAME DU HAUT - WEST EXTERIOR
France, Ronchamp (07 June 1992)
Pen and Ink Drawing on Fabriano Paper
33.02 cm x 48.26 cm (13 in x 19 in)

EUROPE

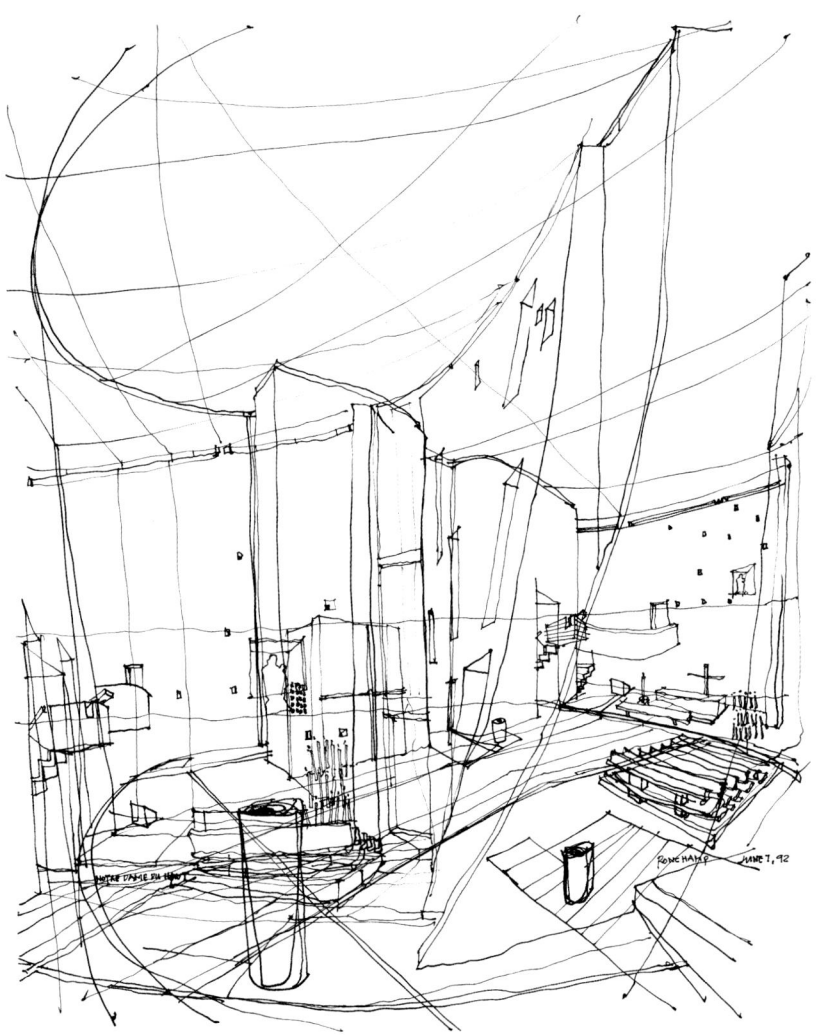

NOTRE DAME DU HAUT - INTERIOR - 02
France, Ronchamp (07 June 1992)
Pen and Ink Drawing on Fabriano Paper
33.02 cm x 48.26 cm (13 in x 19 in)

THE PARADOX OF PLACE: IN THE LINE OF SIGHT

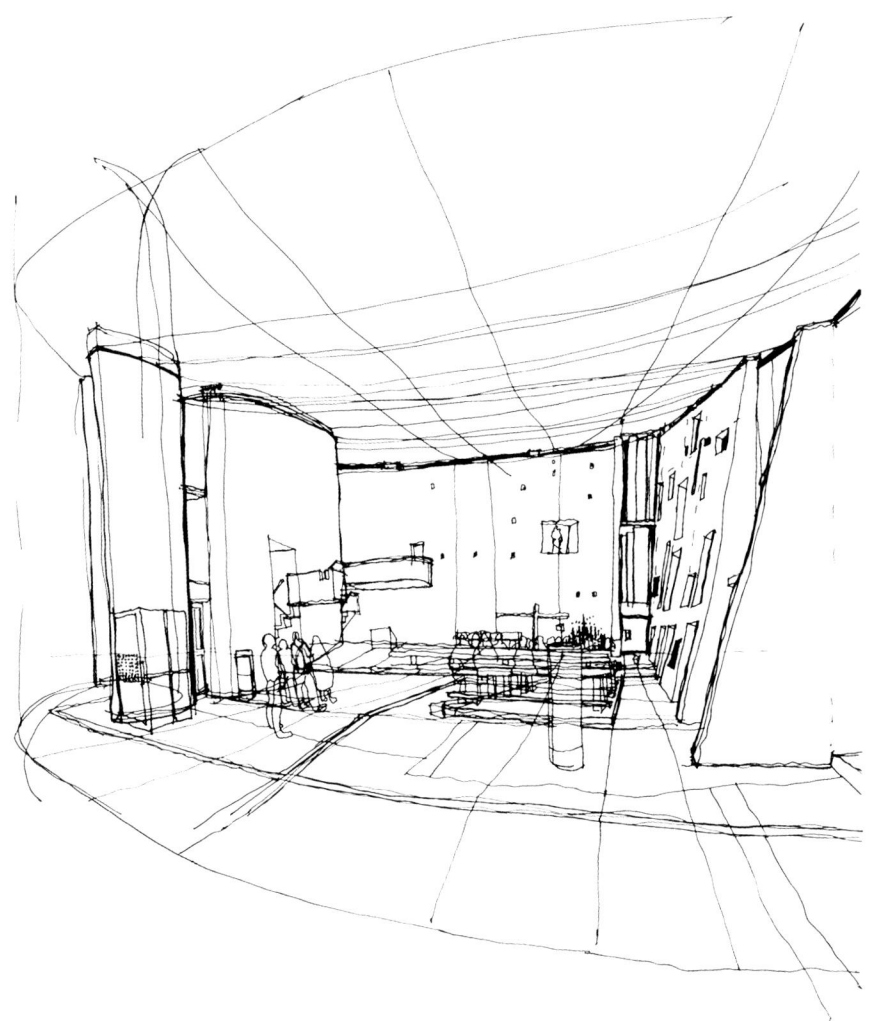

NOTRE DAME DU HAUT - NAVE
France, Ronchamp (07 June 1992)
Pen and Ink Drawing on Fabriano Paper
33.02 cm x 48.26 cm (13 in x 19 in)

EUROPE

NOTRE DAME DU HAUT - OUTDOOR PULPIT
France, Ronchamp (07 June 1992)
Pen and Ink Drawing on Fabriano Paper
33.02 cm x 48.26 cm (13 in x 19 in)

THE PARADOX OF PLACE: IN THE LINE OF SIGHT

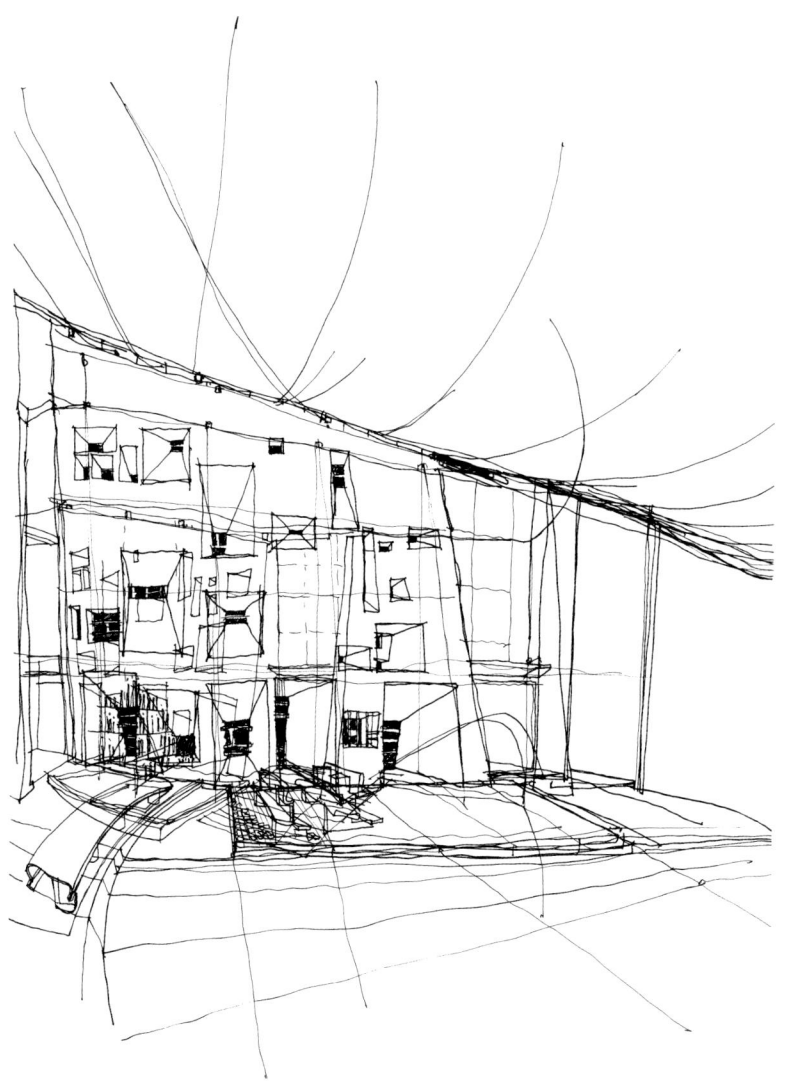

NOTRE DAME DU HAUT - FILL WALL - 01
France, Ronchamp (07 June 1992)
Pen and Ink Drawing on Fabriano Paper
33.02 cm x 48.26 cm (13 in x 19 in)

EUROPE

FERRY FROM GREECE
Greece, Appia (10 August 1973)
Pen and Ink Drawing on Fabriano Paper
33.02 cm x 48.26 cm (13 in x 19 in)

THE PARADOX OF PLACE: IN THE LINE OF SIGHT

PASSAGE - 01
Italy, Assisi (17 June 1992)
Pen and Ink Drawing on Fabriano Paper
33.02 cm x 48.26 cm (13 in x 19 in)

EUROPE

BORGO ARETINO - PORTA SUD
Italy, Assisi (24 July 1987)
Pen and Ink Drawing on Fabriano Paper
33.02 cm x 48.26 cm (13 in x 19 in)

THE PARADOX OF PLACE: IN THE LINE OF SIGHT

PASSAGE VIA S. ANTONIO - PIAZZA VESCOVADO
Italy, Assisi (17 June 1992)
Pen and Ink Drawing on Fabriano Paper
33.02 cm x 48.26 cm (13 in x 19 in)

EUROPE

E-W PASSAGE SCALETA DELLO SPIRITO SANTO - PIAZZATA DI SAN FRANCESCO PICCOLINO
Italy, Assisi (21 June 1991)
Pen and Ink Drawing on Fabriano Paper
33.02 cm x 48.26 cm (13 in x 19 in)

THE PARADOX OF PLACE: IN THE LINE OF SIGHT

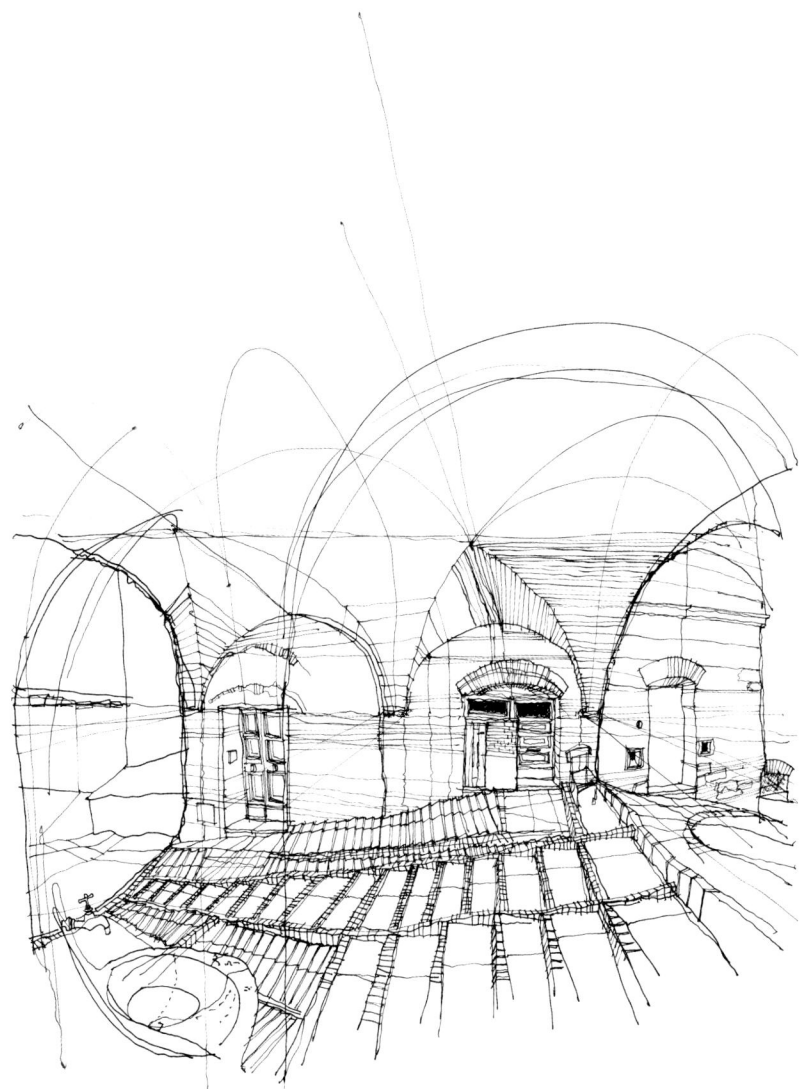

SOTTOPASSAGGIO
Italy, Assisi (21 June 1991)
Pen and Ink Drawing on Fabriano Paper
33.02 cm x 48.26 cm (13 in x 19 in)

EUROPE

PASSAGE - 02
Italy, Assisi (20 November 1992)
Pen and Ink Drawing on Fabriano Paper
33.02 cm x 48.26 cm (13 in x 19 in)

THE PARADOX OF PLACE: IN THE LINE OF SIGHT

CINQUE TERRA - CHIESA SAN PIETRO
Italy, Corniglia (Undated)
Pen and Ink Drawing on Fabriano Paper
33.02 cm x 48.26 cm (13 in x 19 in)

EUROPE

CAFE DELLA VIA - FIRENZE
Italy, Florence (28 July 1979)
Pen and Ink Drawing with Watercolor Wash on Fabriano Paper
33.02 cm x 48.26 cm (13 in x 19 in)

THE PARADOX OF PLACE: IN THE LINE OF SIGHT

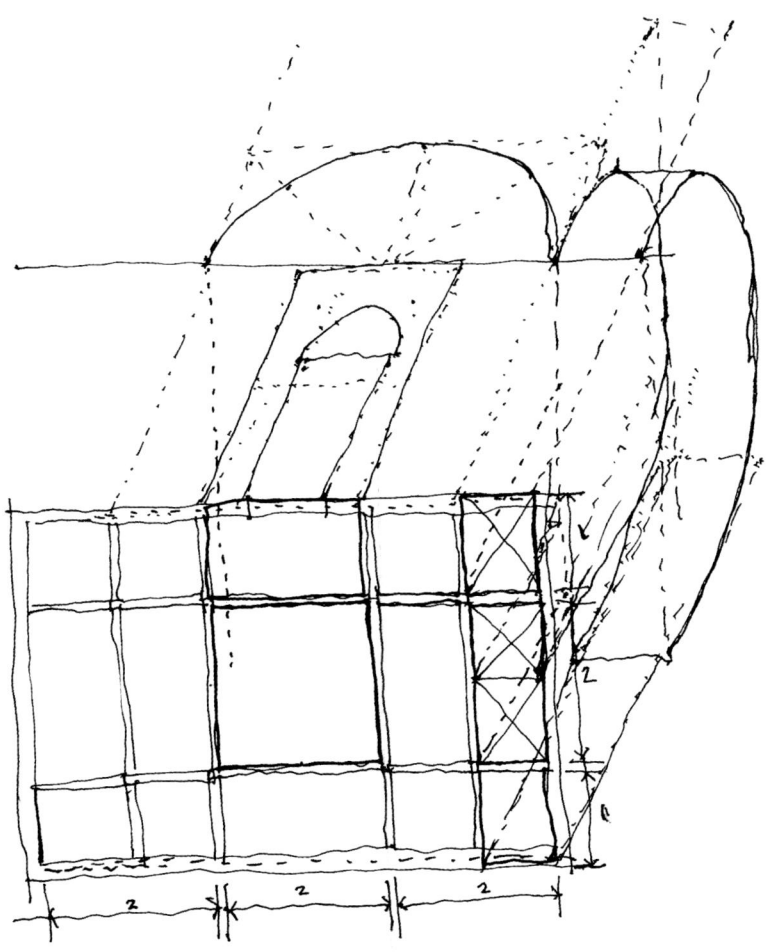

CAPPELLA DEI PAZZI - AXON SKETCH - 01
Italy, Florence (Undated)
Pen and Ink Drawing on Fabriano Paper
33.02 cm x 48.26 cm (13 in x 19 in)

EUROPE

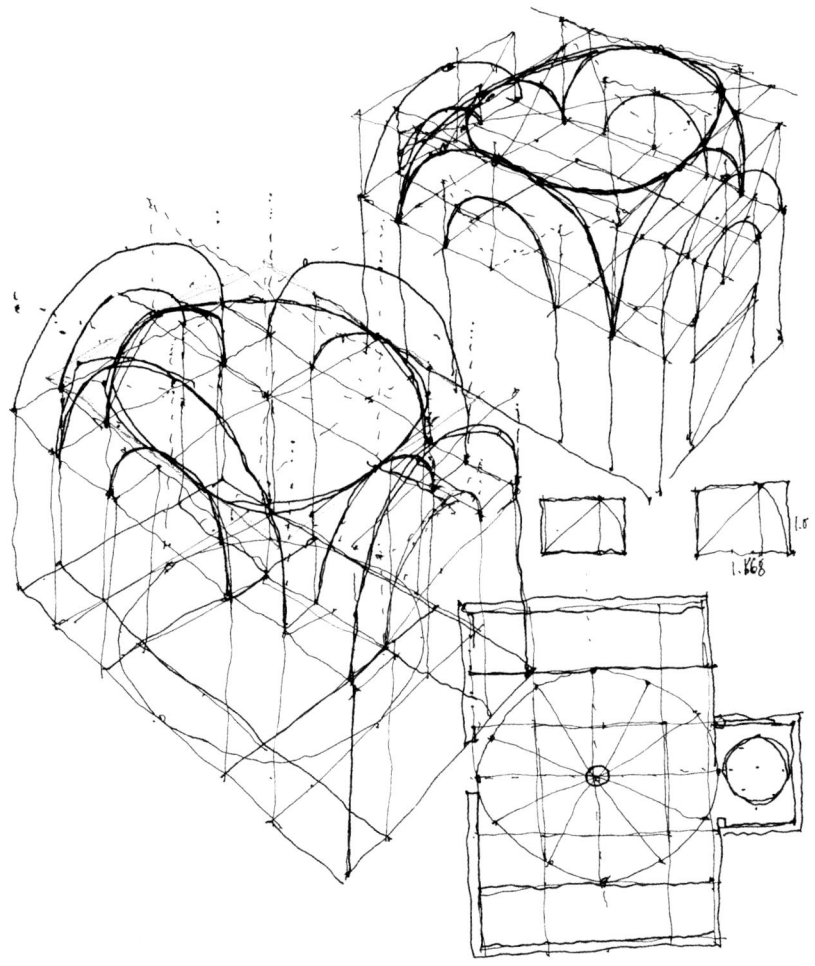

CAPPELLA DEI PAZZI - AXON SKETCH - 02
Italy, Florence (Undated)
Pen and Ink Drawing on Fabriano Paper
33.02 cm x 48.26 cm (13 in x 19 in)

THE PARADOX OF PLACE: IN THE LINE OF SIGHT

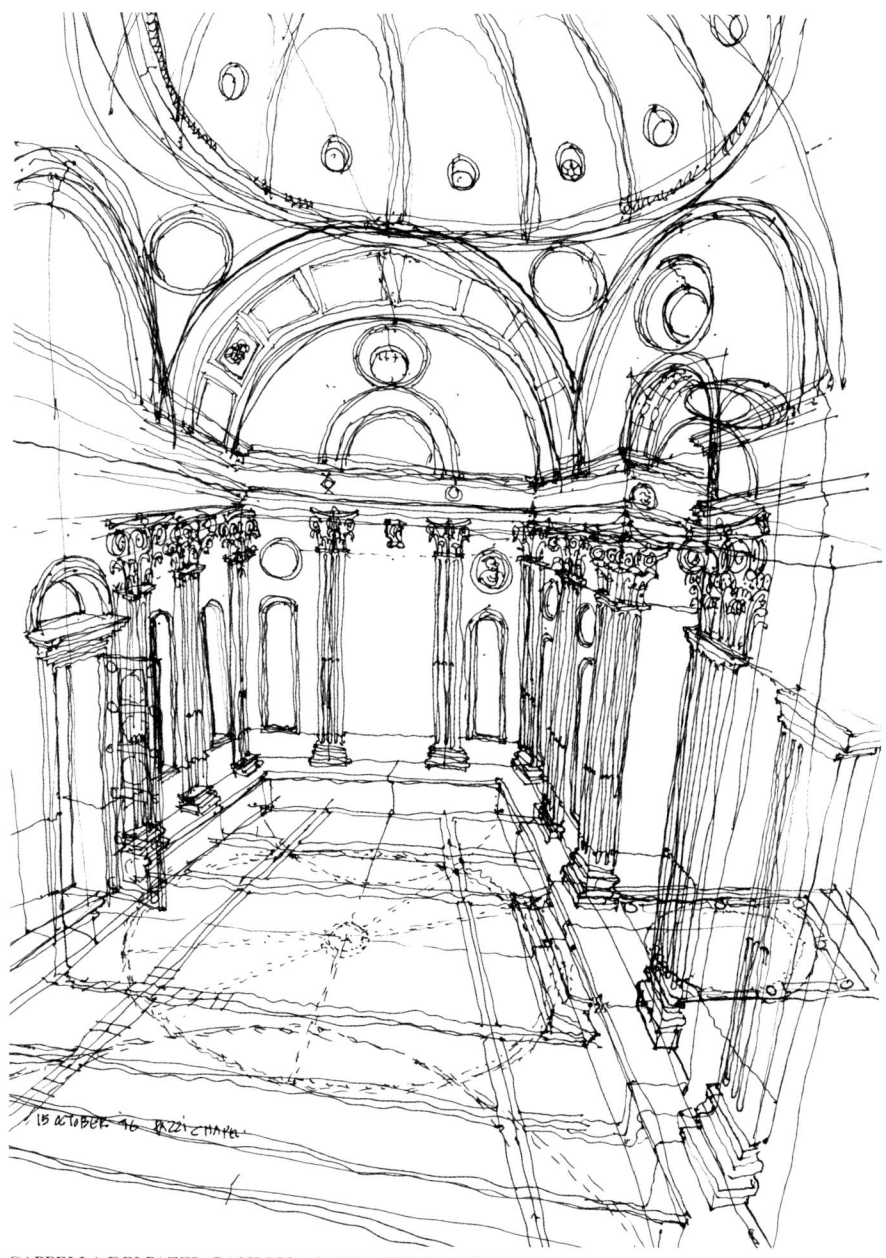

CAPPELLA DEI PAZZI - BASILLICA SANTA CROCE - FIRENZE
Italy, Florence (15 October 1976)
Pen and Ink Drawing on Fabriano Paper
33.02 cm x 48.26 cm (13 in x 19 in)

EUROPE

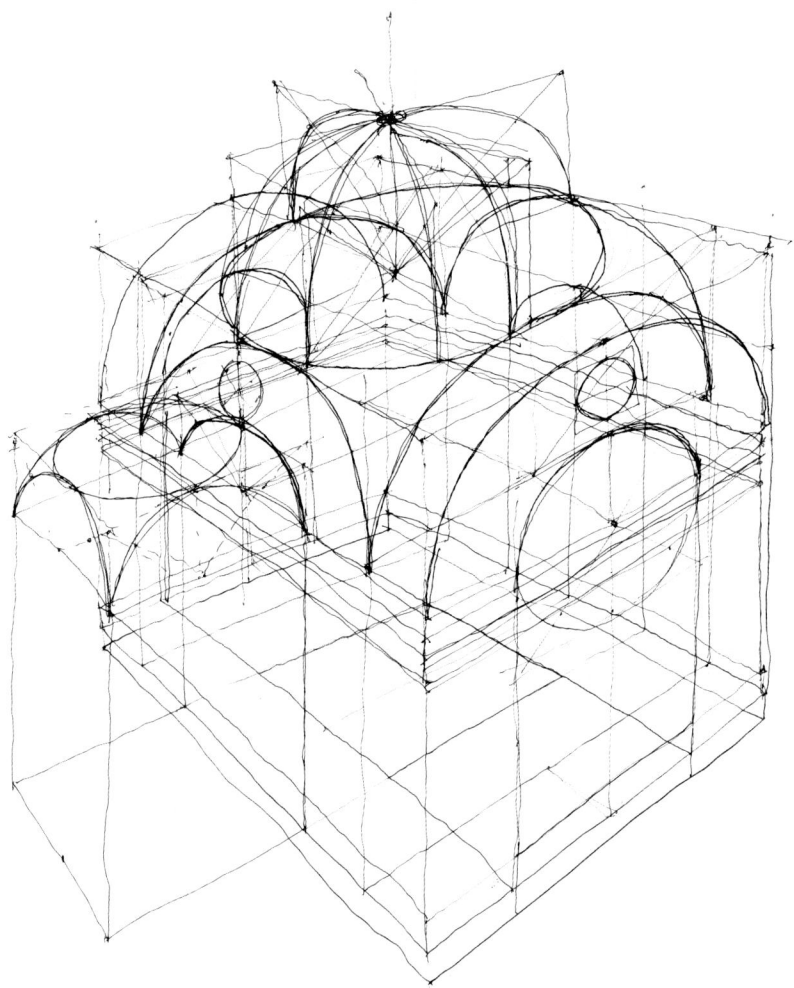

CAPPELLA DEI PAZZI - CAPPELLA PAZZI
Italy, Florence (Undated)
Pen and Ink Drawing on Fabriano Paper
33.02 cm x 48.26 cm (13 in x 19 in)

THE PARADOX OF PLACE: IN THE LINE OF SIGHT

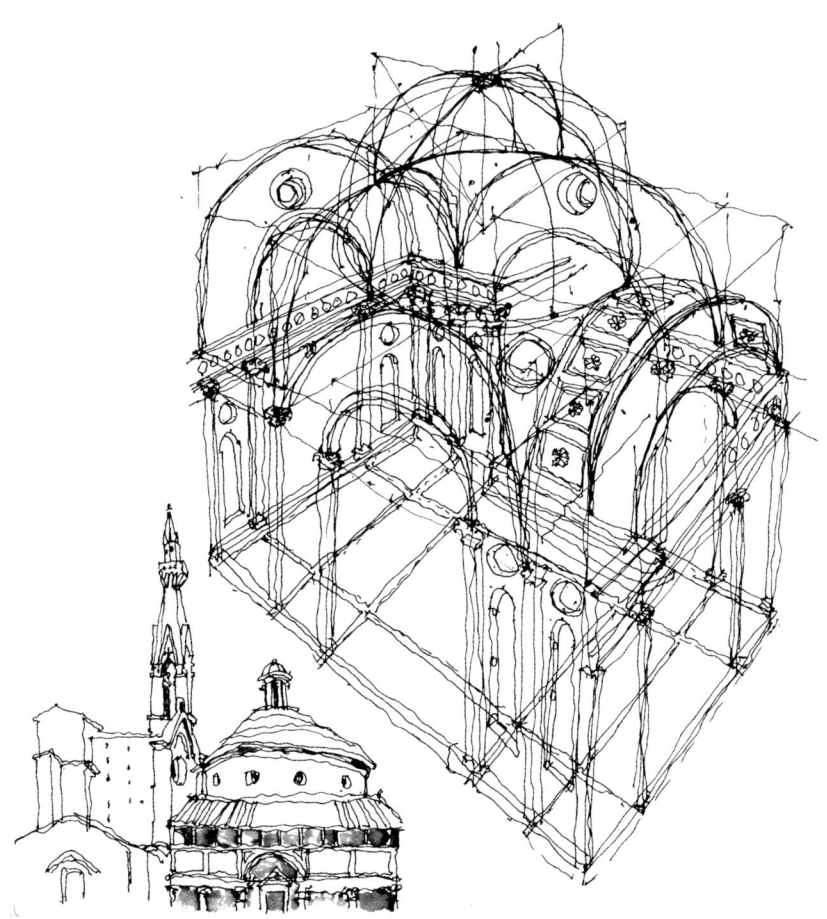

CAPPELLA DEI PAZZI - SANTA CROCE - FIRENZE - 01
Italy, Florence (Undated)
Pen and Ink Drawing with Wash on Fabriano Paper
33.02 cm x 48.26 cm (13 in x 19 in)

EUROPE

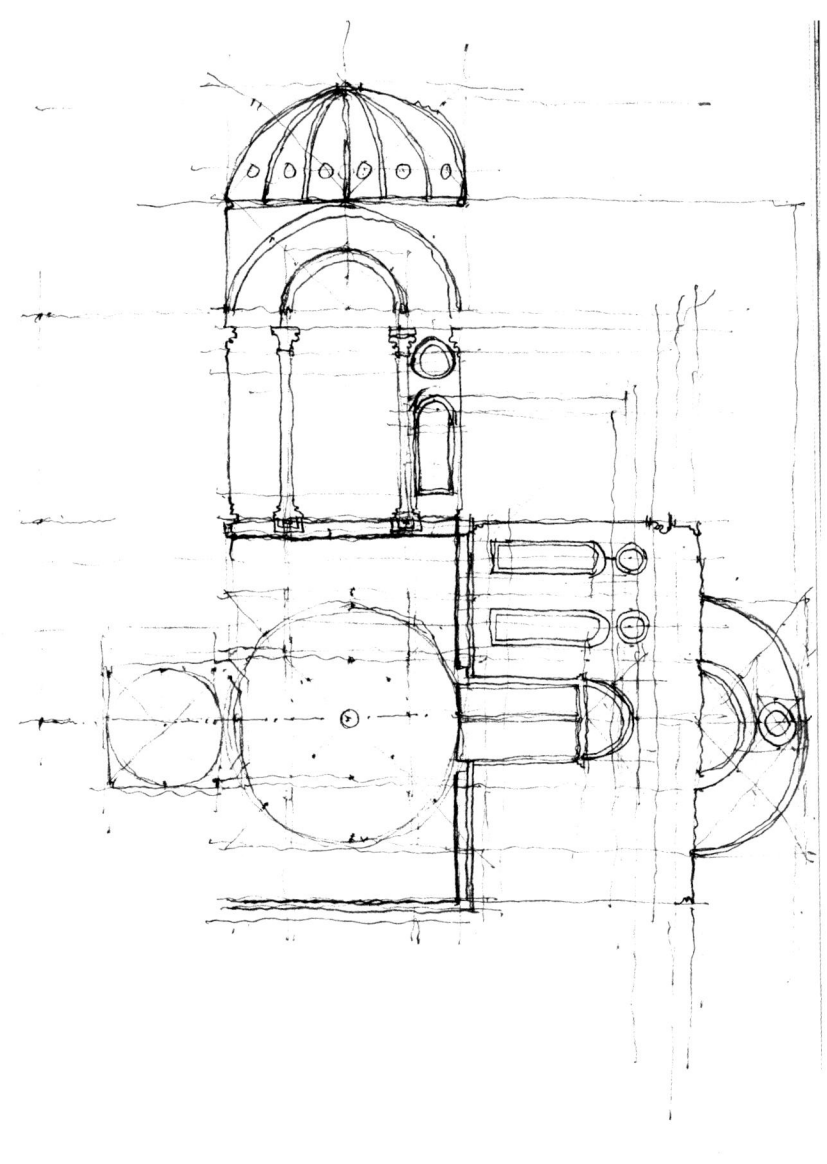

CAPPELLA DEI PAZZI - SANATA CROCE - FIRENZE - 02
Italy, Florence (Undated)
Pen and Ink Drawing on Fabriano Paper
33.02 cm x 48.26 cm (13 in x 19 in)

THE PARADOX OF PLACE: IN THE LINE OF SIGHT

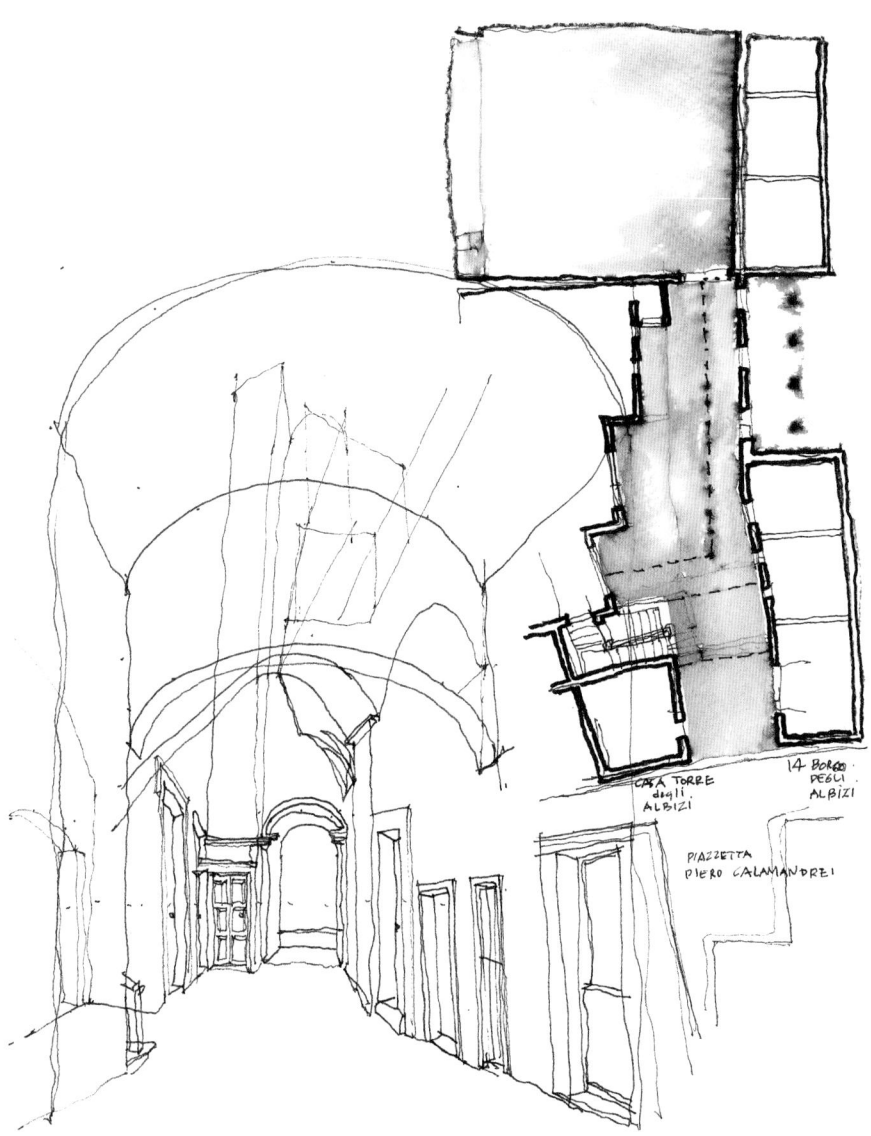

CASA TORRE DEGLI ALBIZI I - FIRENZE - 01
Italy, Florence (Undated)
Pen and Ink Drawing with Wash on Fabriano Paper
33.02 cm x 48.26 cm (13 in x 19 in)

EUROPE

CASA TORRE DEGLI ALBIZI II - FIRENZE - 02
Italy, Florence (Undated)
Pen and Ink Drawing with Wash on Fabriano Paper
33.02 cm x 48.26 cm (13 in x 19 in)

THE PARADOX OF PLACE: IN THE LINE OF SIGHT

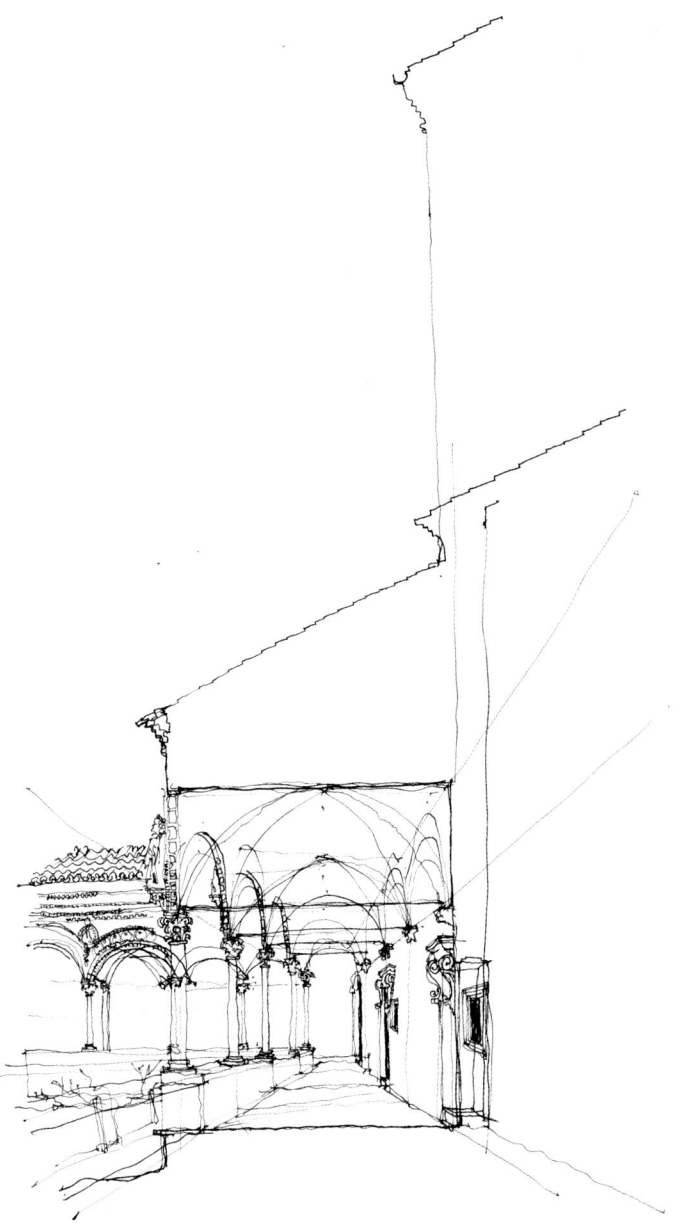

CERTOSA DEL GALLUZZO - 01
Italy, Florence (Undated)
Pen and Ink Drawing on Fabriano Paper
33.02 cm x 48.26 cm (13 in x 19 in)

EUROPE

CHIESA DI SANTA MARGHERITA DEI CERCHI - FIRENZE - 01
Italy, Florence (Undated)
Pen and Ink Drawing on Fabriano Paper
33.02 cm x 48.26 cm (13 in x 19 in)

THE PARADOX OF PLACE: IN THE LINE OF SIGHT

CHIOSTRO SAN LORENZO - BIBLIOTECA MEDICEA LAURENZIANA - 01
Italy, Florence (October 1996)
Pen and Ink Drawing on Fabriano Paper
33.02 cm x 48.26 cm (13 in x 19 in)

EUROPE

CHIOSTRO SAN LORENZO - IL CHIOSTRO DEI CANONICI - BIBLIOTECA MEDICEA LAURENZIANA
Italy, Florence (October 1996)
Pen and Ink Drawing on Fabriano Paper
33.02 cm x 48.26 cm (13 in x 19 in)

THE PARADOX OF PLACE: IN THE LINE OF SIGHT

FIRENZA - DUOMO VIEW VIA DEL STUDIO - 01
Italy, Florence (Undated)
Pen and Ink Drawing on Fabriano Paper
33.02 cm x 48.26 cm (13 in x 19 in)

EUROPE

SANTO SPIRITO - BORGO OLTRARNO
Italy, Florence (Undated)
Pen and Ink Drawing with Watercolor Wash on Fabriano Paper
33.02 cm x 48.26 cm (13 in x 19 in)

THE PARADOX OF PLACE: IN THE LINE OF SIGHT

FIRENZA - TRATTORIA - IL CAMINETTO
Italy, Florence (Undated)
Pen and Ink Drawing on Fabriano Paper
33.02 cm x 48.26 cm (13 in x 19 in)

EUROPE

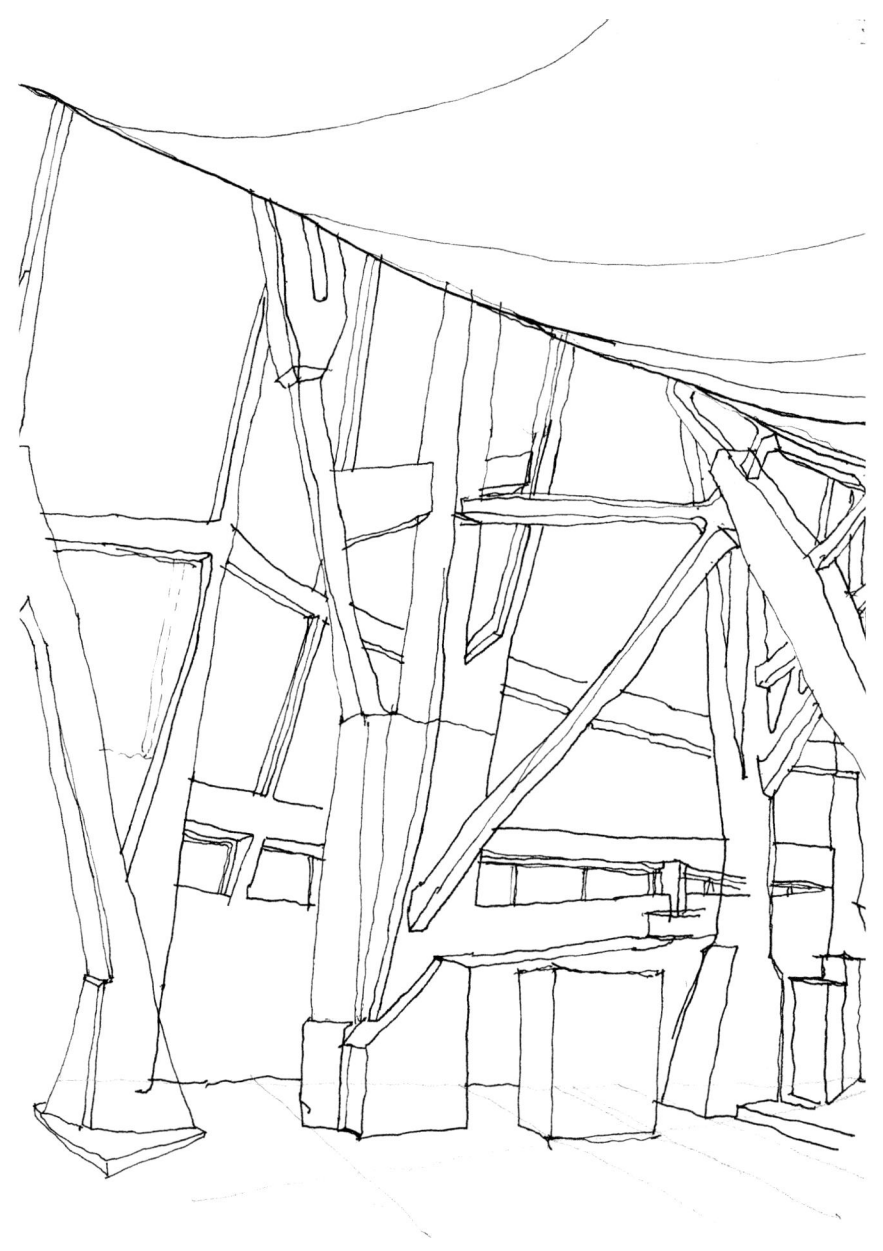

SAN GIOVANNI BATTISTA - FIRENZE - 01
Italy, Florence (Undated
Pen and Ink Drawing on Fabriano Paper
33.02 cm x 48.26 cm (13 in x 19 in)

THE PARADOX OF PLACE: IN THE LINE OF SIGHT

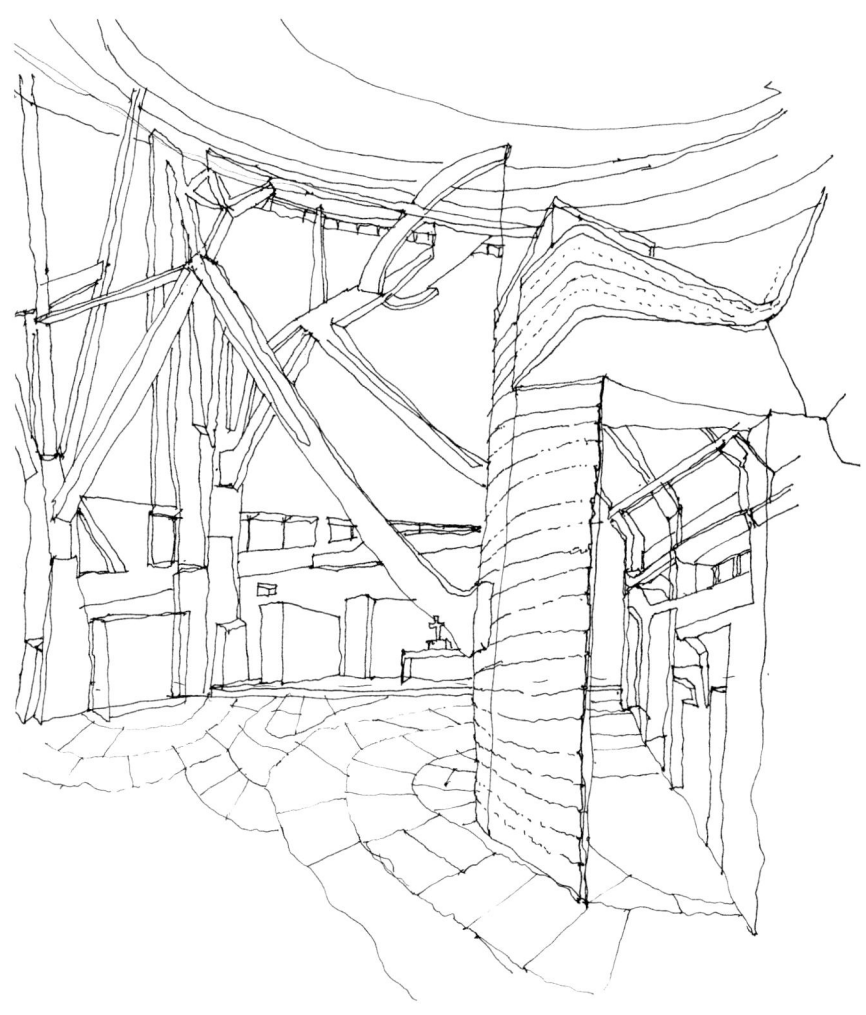

SAN GIOVANNI BATTISTA - FIRENZE - 02
Italy, Florence (Undated)
Pen and Ink Drawing on Fabriano Paper
33.02 cm x 48.26 cm (13 in x 19 in)

EUROPE

PIAZZA D'ERBE
Italy, Mantova (18 July 1977)
Pen and Ink Drawing with Wash on Fabriano Paper; Pen and Ink Drawing on Fabriano Paper
33.02 cm x 48.26 cm (13 in x 19 in)

THE PARADOX OF PLACE: IN THE LINE OF SIGHT

ORVIETTO YARIS
Italy, Mantova (25 July 1977)
Pen and Ink Drawing with Wash on Fabriano Paper; Pen and Ink Drawing on Fabriano Paper
33.02 cm x 48.26 cm (13 in x 19 in)

EUROPE

CEMITERIO DE SAN CATALDO - 01
Italy, Modena (Undated)
Pen and Ink Drawing on Fabriano Paper
33.02 cm x 48.26 cm (13 in x 19 in)

THE PARADOX OF PLACE: IN THE LINE OF SIGHT

CEMITERIO DE SAN CATALDO - 02
Italy, Modena (October 2002)
Pen and Ink Drawing on Fabriano Paper
33.02 cm x 48.26 cm (13 in x 19 in)

EUROPE

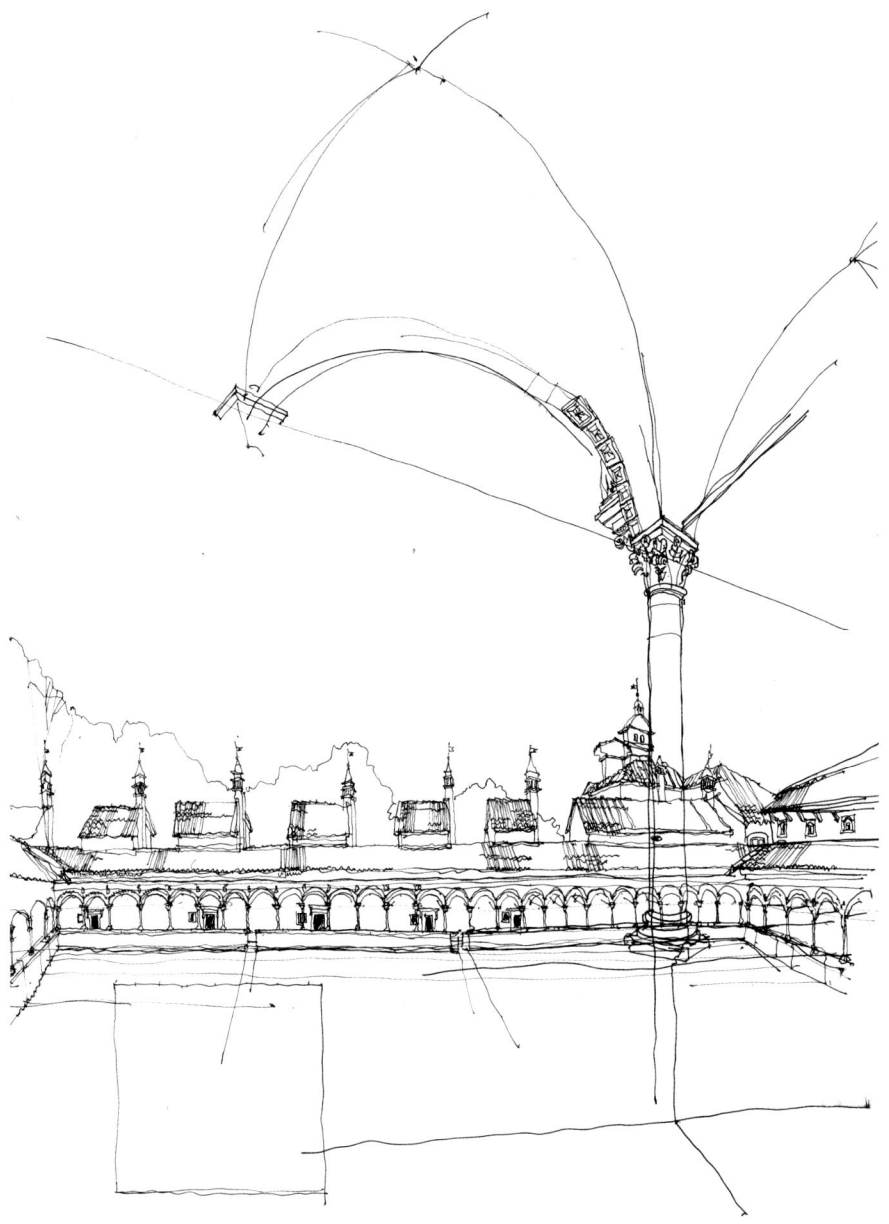

CERTOSA DI PAVIA - 01
Italy, Pavia (September 2001)
Pen and Ink Drawing on Fabriano Paper
33.02 cm x 48.26 cm (13 in x 19 in)

THE PARADOX OF PLACE: IN THE LINE OF SIGHT

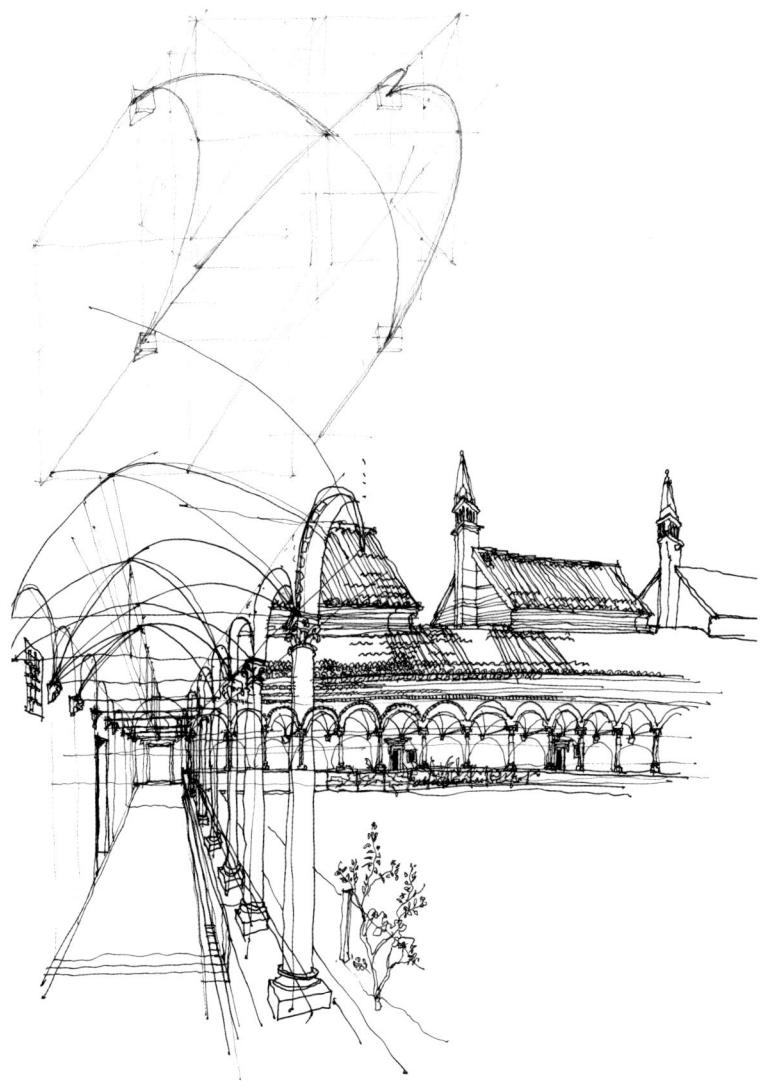

CERTOSA DI PAVIA - 02
Italy, Pavia (September 2001)
Pen and Ink Drawing on Fabriano Paper
33.02 cm x 48.26 cm (13 in x 19 in)

EUROPE

CENTRO STORICO SOPRA - PORTA DI SANTA MARGHERITA - EAST EDGE
Italy, Perugia (Undated)
Pen and Ink Drawing on Fabriano Paper
33.02 cm x 48.26 cm (13 in x 19 in)

THE PARADOX OF PLACE: IN THE LINE OF SIGHT

PALAZZO DEI PRIORI DAL CATTEDRALE DI SAN LORENZO - 01
Italy, Perugia (Undated)
Pen and Ink Drawing with Pencil on Fabriano Paper
33.02 cm x 48.26 cm (13 in x 19 in)

EUROPE

PIAZZA PIO II
Italy, Pienza (2006)
Pen and Ink Drawing on Fabriano Paper
33.02 cm x 48.26 cm (13 in x 19 in)

THE PARADOX OF PLACE: IN THE LINE OF SIGHT

PICCOLO STRADE A PIAZZO PIO - 02
Italy, Pienza (2006)
Pen and Ink Drawing on Fabriano Paper
33.02 cm x 48.26 cm (13 in x 19 in)

EUROPE

CALLE DI GROSSETO
Italy, Pitgliano (Undated)
Pen and Ink Drawing on Fabriano Paper
33.02 cm x 48.26 cm (13 in x 19 in)

THE PARADOX OF PLACE: IN THE LINE OF SIGHT

PONTITO - 01
Italy, Pontito (Undated)
Pen and Ink Drawing on Fabriano Paper
33.02 cm x 48.26 cm (13 in x 19 in)

EUROPE

CINQUE TERRA - RIOMAGGIORE
Italy, Riomaggiore (October 2001)
Pen and Ink Drawing on Fabriano Paper
33.02 cm x 48.26 cm (13 in x 19 in)

THE PARADOX OF PLACE: IN THE LINE OF SIGHT

CHIESA SAN GIOVANNI BATTISTA DEI FIORENTINI - ALTARE
Italy, Rome (Undated)
Pen and Ink Drawing with Pencil on Fabriano Paper
33.02 cm x 48.26 cm (13 in x 19 in)

EUROPE

CHIESA SAN GIOVANNI BATTISTA DEI FIORENTINI - PULPITO
Italy, Rome (Undated)
Pen and Ink Drawing with Pencil on Fabriano Paper
33.02 cm x 48.26 cm (13 in x 19 in)

THE PARADOX OF PLACE: IN THE LINE OF SIGHT

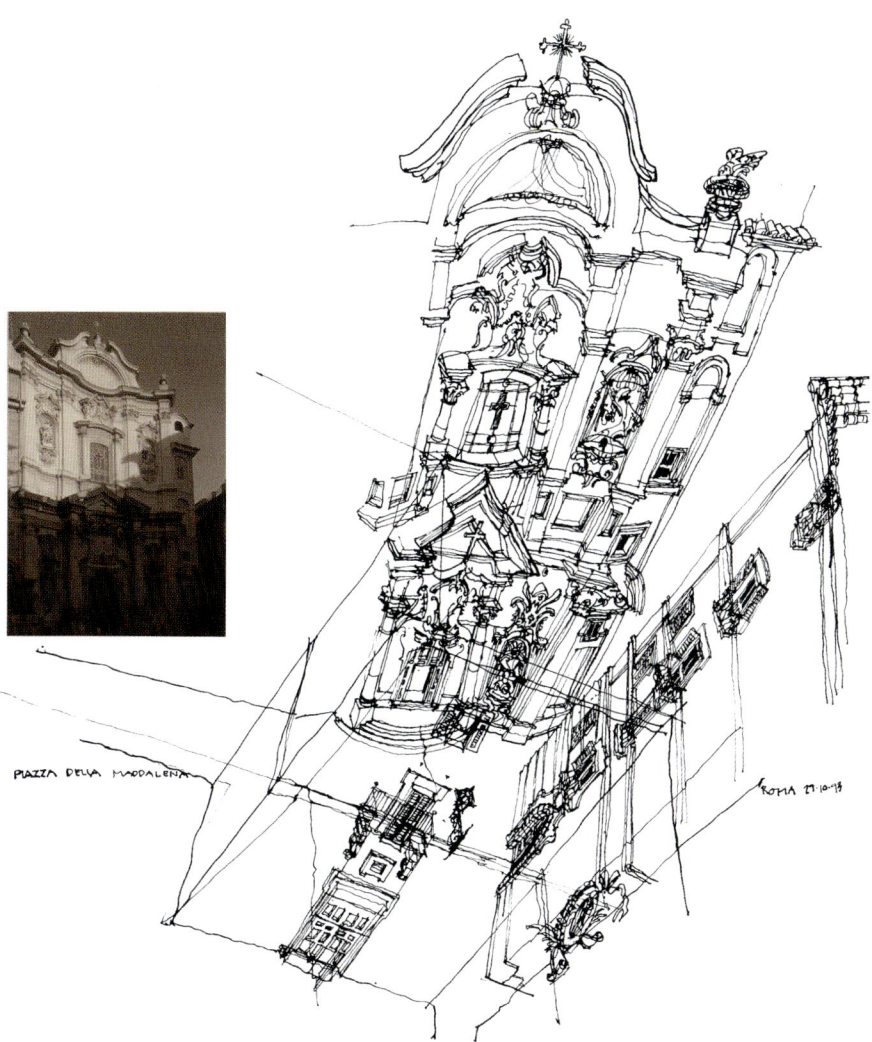

PIAZZA DELLA MADDALENA - 01
Italy, Rome (29 October 1993)
Inset Photograph; Pen and Ink Drawing on Fabriano Paper
33.02 cm x 48.26 cm (13 in x 19 in)

EUROPE

PICOLO PASSAGIO - P. BISCIONE - 01
Italy, Rome (Undated)
Pen and Ink Drawing on Fabriano Paper
33.02 cm x 48.26 cm (13 in x 19 in)

THE PARADOX OF PLACE: IN THE LINE OF SIGHT

SAN GIMIGNANO - 01
Italy, San Gimignano (Undated)
Pen and Ink Drawing on Fabriano Paper
33.02 cm x 48.26 cm (13 in x 19 in)

EUROPE

PIAZZA CISTERNA - SAN GIMIGNANO
Italy, San Gimignano (Undated)
Pen and Ink Drawing with Watercolor Wash on Fabriano Paper
33.02 cm x 48.26 cm (13 in x 19 in)

THE PARADOX OF PLACE: IN THE LINE OF SIGHT

PIAZZA DEL DUOMO
Italy, San Gimignano (Undated)
Pen and Ink Drawing with Watercolor Wash on Fabriano Paper
33.02 cm x 48.26 cm (13 in x 19 in)

EUROPE

PIAZZA DEL DUOMO - PALAZZO DEL PODESTA
Italy, San Gimignano (Undated)
Pen and Ink Drawing on Fabriano Paper
33.02 cm x 48.26 cm (13 in x 19 in)

THE PARADOX OF PLACE: IN THE LINE OF SIGHT

PIAZZA DEL DUOMO - PALAZZO VECCHIO DEL PODESTA
Italy, Pontito (Undated)
Pen and Ink Drawing on Fabriano Paper
33.02 cm x 48.26 cm (13 in x 19 in)

EUROPE

SAN GIMIGNANO
Italy, San Gimignano (Undated)
Pen and Ink Drawing on Fabriano Paper
33.02 cm x 48.26 cm (13 in x 19 in)

THE PARADOX OF PLACE: IN THE LINE OF SIGHT

VIA S. MATTEO
Italy, San Gimignano (Undated)
Pen and Ink Drawing on Fabriano Paper
33.02 cm x 48.26 cm (13 in x 19 in)

EUROPE

CIMITERO BRION - 01
Italy, San Vito d'Altivole (Undated)
Pen and Ink Drawing with Watercolor Wash on Fabriano Paper
33.02 cm x 48.26 cm (13 in x 19 in)

THE PARADOX OF PLACE: IN THE LINE OF SIGHT

CIMITERO BRION - 02
Italy, San Vito d'Altivole (Undated)
Pen and Ink Drawing with Watercolor Wash on Fabriano Paper
33.02 cm x 48.26 cm (13 in x 19 in)

EUROPE

CIMITERO BRION - 03
Italy, San Vito d'Altivole (Undated)
Pen and Ink Drawing on Fabriano Paper
33.02 cm x 48.26 cm (13 in x 19 in)

THE PARADOX OF PLACE: IN THE LINE OF SIGHT

APPROACHING IL DUOMO - 01
Italy, Siena (Undated)
Pen and Ink Drawing on Fabriano Paper
33.02 cm x 48.26 cm (13 in x 19 in)

EUROPE

BORDO DELL IL CAMPO - 01
Italy, Siena (Undated)
Pen and Ink Drawing on Fabriano Paper
33.02 cm x 48.26 cm (13 in x 19 in)

THE PARADOX OF PLACE: IN THE LINE OF SIGHT

PASSAGE VIA DI PELLEGRINI
Italy, Siena (Undated)
Pen and Ink Drawing on Fabriano Paper
33.02 cm x 48.26 cm (13 in x 19 in)

EUROPE

VICOLO DEL VANNELLO
Italy, Siena (Undated)
Pen and Ink Drawing on Fabriano Paper
33.02 cm x 48.26 cm (13 in x 19 in)

THE PARADOX OF PLACE: IN THE LINE OF SIGHT

CAMPO PASSAGE VICOLO DEL VANNELLO
Italy, Siena (13 November 1991)
Pen and Ink Drawing on Fabriano Paper
33.02 cm x 48.26 cm (13 in x 19 in)

EUROPE

DUOMO
Italy, Siena (Undated)
Pen and Ink Drawing on Fabriano Paper
33.02 cm x 48.26 cm (13 in x 19 in)

THE PARADOX OF PLACE: IN THE LINE OF SIGHT

IL CAMPO
Italy, Siena (Undated)
Pen and Ink Drawing with Watercolor Wash and Color Pencil on Fabriano Paper
33.02 cm x 48.26 cm (13 in x 19 in)

EUROPE

PASSAGGI DELL INTERSEZIONE QUARTTO
Italy, Siena (20 June 1992)
Pen and Ink Drawing on Fabriano Paper
33.02 cm x 48.26 cm (13 in x 19 in)

102

THE PARADOX OF PLACE: IN THE LINE OF SIGHT

S. CRISTIFORO
Italy, Siena (20 June 1992)
Pen and Ink Drawing on Fabriano Paper
33.02 cm x 48.26 cm (13 in x 19 in)

EUROPE

STREET ADDRESS
Italy, Siena (Undated)
Pen and Ink Drawing on Fabriano Paper
33.02 cm x 48.26 cm (13 in x 19 in)

THE PARADOX OF PLACE: IN THE LINE OF SIGHT

S. AUGUSTINO
Italy, Siena (13 November 1991)
Pen and Ink Drawing on Fabriano Paper
33.02 cm x 48.26 cm (13 in x 19 in)

EUROPE

VICOLO DI SAN PIETRO DALL IL CAMPO
Italy, Siena (12 June 1992)
Pen and Ink Drawing on Fabriano Paper
33.02 cm x 48.26 cm (13 in x 19 in)

THE PARADOX OF PLACE: IN THE LINE OF SIGHT

CITTÀ DELLA COLLINA
Italy, Stiappa (Undated)
Pen and Ink Drawing on Fabriano Paper
33.02 cm x 48.26 cm (13 in x 19 in)

EUROPE

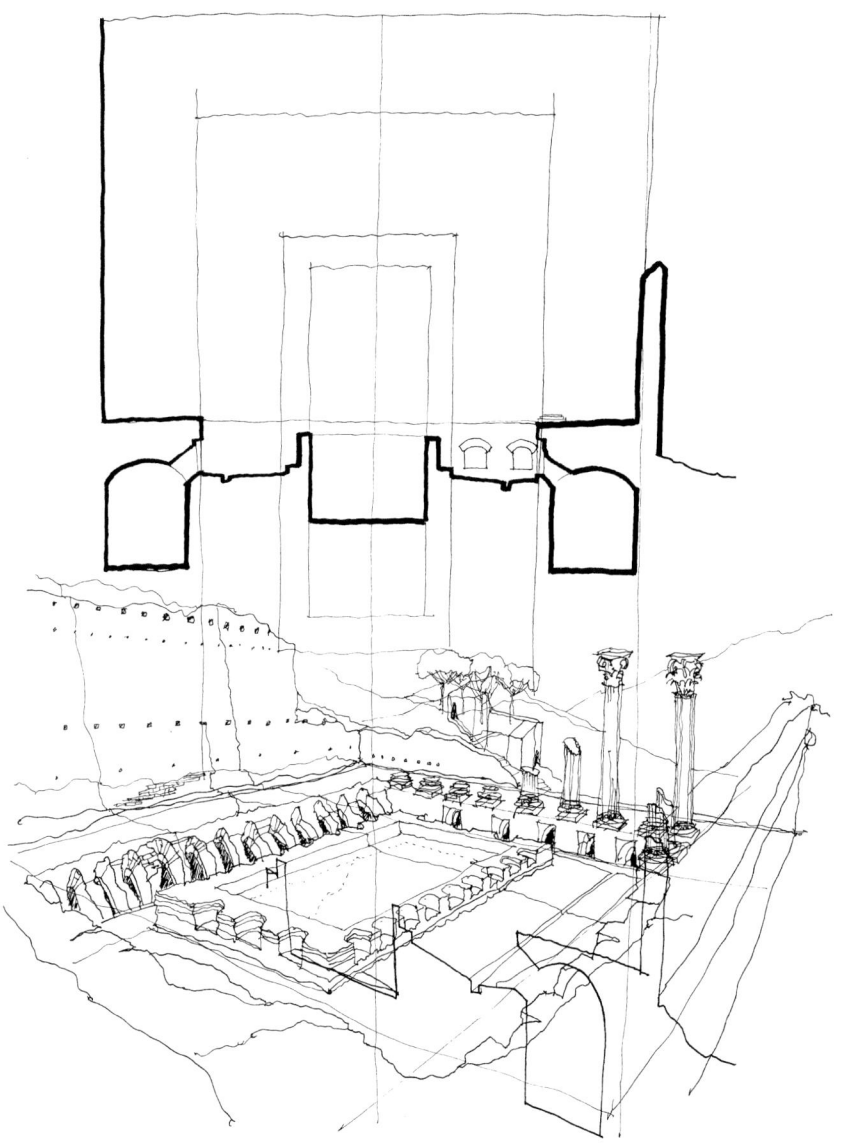

VILLA ADRIANA - POOL PASSAGE
Italy, Tivoli (Undated)
Pen and Ink Drawing on Fabriano Paper
33.02 cm x 48.26 cm (13 in x 19 in)

THE PARADOX OF PLACE: IN THE LINE OF SIGHT

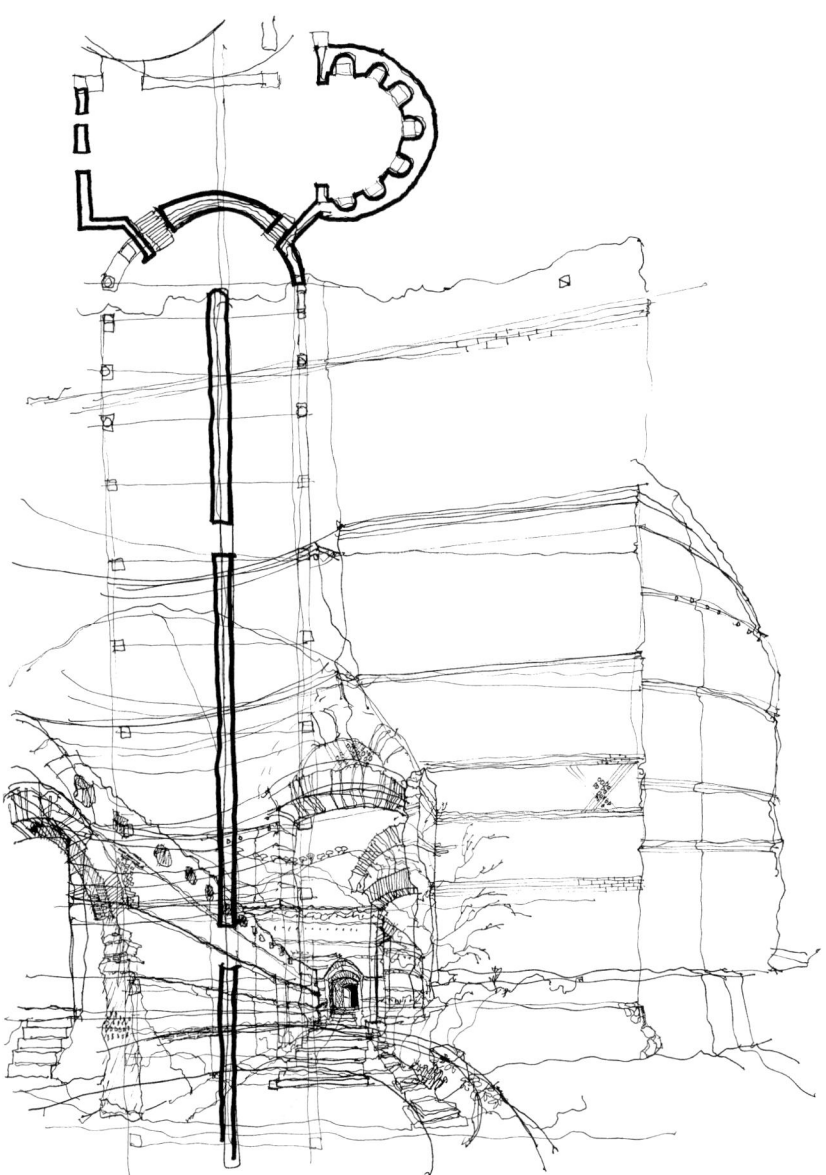

VILLA ADRIANA - VILLA ENTRY
Italy, Tivoli (Undated)
Pen and Ink Drawing on Fabriano Paper
33.02 cm x 48.26 cm (13 in x 19 in)

EUROPE

VILLA ADRIANA - CORTILE PALAZZO
Italy, Tivoli (20 June 1997)
Pen and Ink Drawing on Fabriano Paper
33.02 cm x 48.26 cm (13 in x 19 in)

THE PARADOX OF PLACE: IN THE LINE OF SIGHT

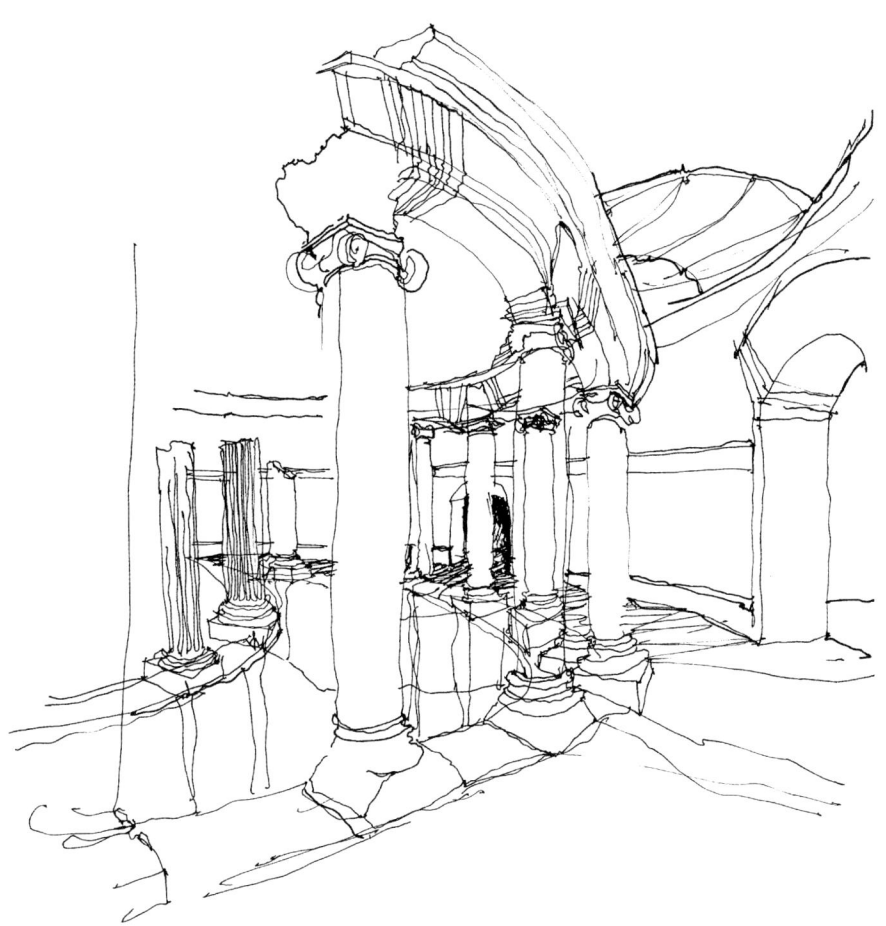

VILLA ADRIANA - MARITIME THEATER
Italy, Tivoli (Undated)
Pen and Ink Drawing on Fabriano Paper
33.02 cm x 48.26 cm (13 in x 19 in)

EUROPE

VILLA ADRIANA - VILLA - 01
Italy, Tivoli (Undated)
Pen and Ink Drawing on Fabriano Paper
33.02 cm x 48.26 cm (13 in x 19 in)

THE PARADOX OF PLACE: IN THE LINE OF SIGHT

VILLA ADRIANA - TRICLINIUM - 02
Italy, Tivoli (Undated)
Pen and Ink Drawing on Fabriano Paper
33.02 cm x 48.26 cm (13 in x 19 in)

EUROPE

VILLA ADRIANA - VILLA CANOPAS
Italy, Tivoli (June 1998)
Pen and Ink Drawing on Fabriano Paper
33.02 cm x 48.26 cm (13 in x 19 in)

THE PARADOX OF PLACE: IN THE LINE OF SIGHT

VILLA ADRIANA - TERNE CON HELIO CAMINUS - 01
Italy, Tivoli (Undated)
Pen and Ink Drawing on Fabriano Paper
33.02 cm x 48.26 cm (13 in x 19 in)

EUROPE

VILLA ADRIANA - TERNE CON HELIO CAMINUS - 02
Italy, Tivoli (October 1996)
Pen and Ink Drawing on Fabriano Paper
33.02 cm x 48.26 cm (13 in x 19 in)

THE PARADOX OF PLACE: IN THE LINE OF SIGHT

ANONOMUS - VENEZIA - 01
Italy, Venice (Undated)
Pen and Ink Drawing on Fabriano Paper
33.02 cm x 48.26 cm (13 in x 19 in)

EUROPE

CALLE ZANE I TO CAMPIELLO S. GIOVANNI - 01
Italy, Venice (Undated)
Pen and Ink Drawing on Fabriano Paper
33.02 cm x 48.26 cm (13 in x 19 in)

THE PARADOX OF PLACE: IN THE LINE OF SIGHT

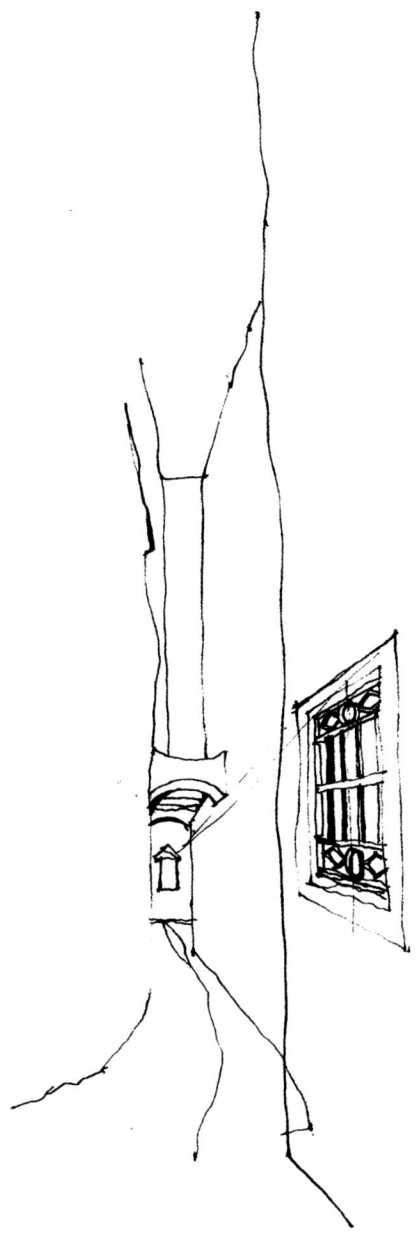

CALLE ZANE II TO CAMPIELLO S. GIOVANNI - 02
Italy, Venice (Undated)
Pen and Ink Drawing on Fabriano Paper
33.02 cm x 48.26 cm (13 in x 19 in)

EUROPE

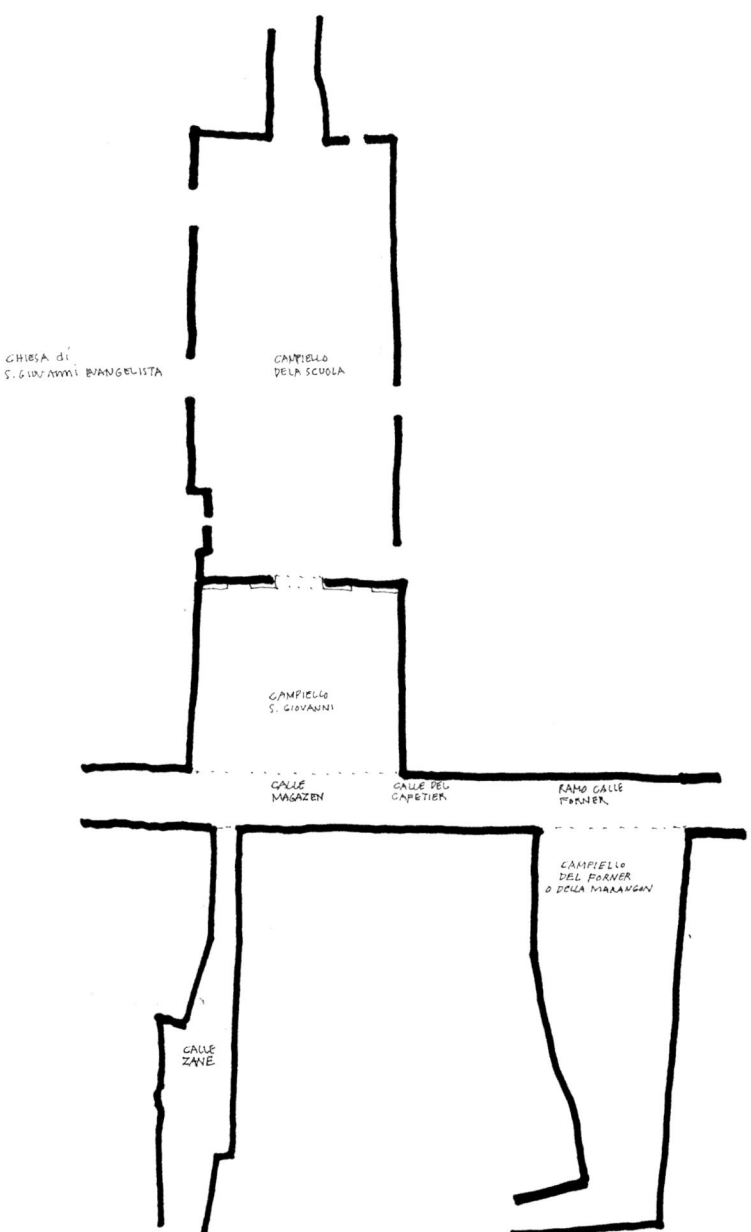

CAMPIELLO S. GIOVANNI - 03
Italy, Venice (Undated)
Pen and Ink Drawing on Fabriano Paper
33.02 cm x 48.26 cm (13 in x 19 in)

THE PARADOX OF PLACE: IN THE LINE OF SIGHT

CANAL - DORSODURO - 01
Italy, Venice (Undated)
Pencil Drawing on Fabriano Paper
33.02 cm x 48.26 cm (13 in x 19 in)

EUROPE

PORTO CAMPIELLO S. GIOVANNI
Italy, Venice (Undated)
Pencil Drawing on Fabriano Paper
33.02 cm x 48.26 cm (13 in x 19 in)

THE PARADOX OF PLACE: IN THE LINE OF SIGHT

VENEZIA - 01
Italy, Venice (Undated)
Pen and Ink Drawing on Fabriano Paper
33.02 cm x 48.26 cm (13 in x 19 in)

EUROPE

PIAZZA SAN MARCO - INTERACTIONS
Italy, Venice (18 August 1974)
Pen and Ink Drawing on Fabriano Paper
33.02 cm x 48.26 cm (13 in x 19 in)

THE PARADOX OF PLACE: IN THE LINE OF SIGHT

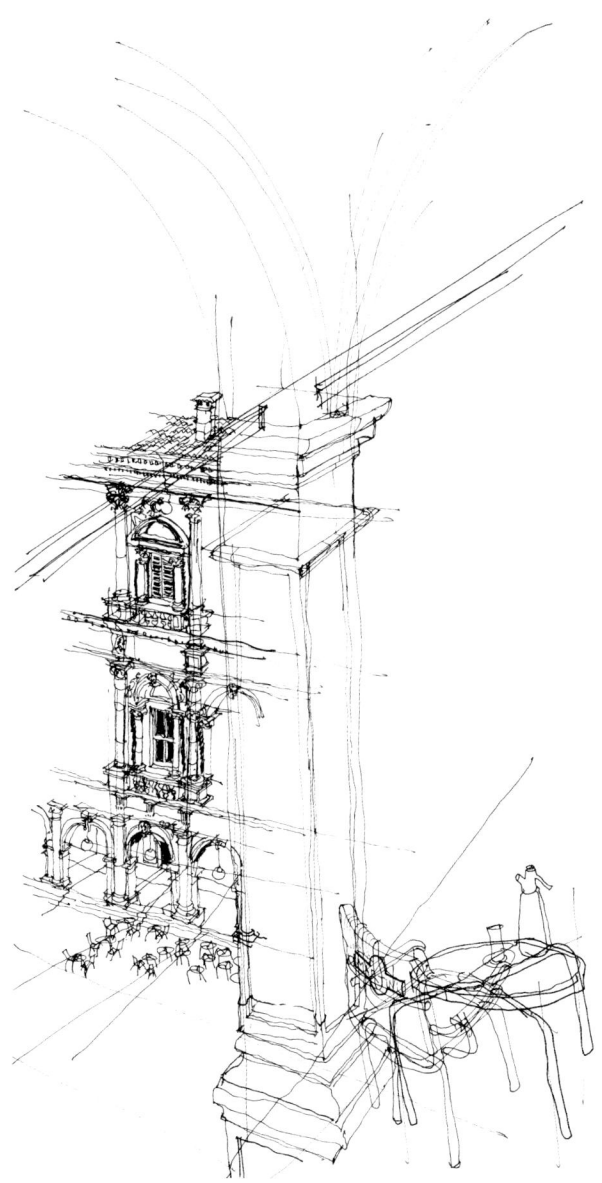

PIAZZA SAN MARCO - 01
Italy, Venice (Undated)
Pen and Ink Drawing on Fabriano Paper
33.02 cm x 48.26 cm (13 in x 19 in)

EUROPE

GONDOLA IN VENICE
Italy, Venice (18 August 1974)
Pen and Ink Drawing on Fabriano Paper
33.02 cm x 48.26 cm (13 in x 19 in)

THE PARADOX OF PLACE: IN THE LINE OF SIGHT

VENEZIA - GRAND CANAL / PONTE RIALTO / VENICE
Italy, Venice (18 August 1978)
Pen and Ink Drawing on Fabriano Paper
33.02 cm x 48.26 cm (13 in x 19 in)

EUROPE

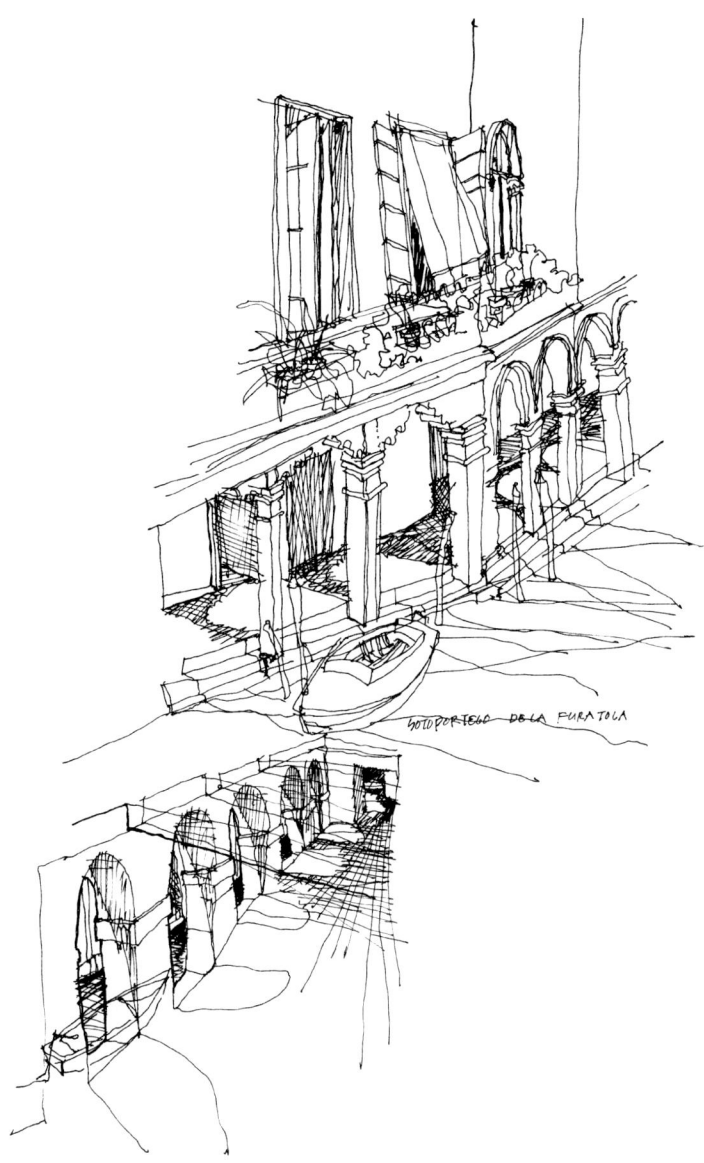

VENEZIA - SOTOPORTEGO DE LA FURATOLA
Italy, Venice (Undated)
Pen and Ink Drawing on Fabriano Paper
33.02 cm x 48.26 cm (13 in x 19 in)

THE PARADOX OF PLACE: IN THE LINE OF SIGHT

BASILICA DI SANTA MARIA DELLA SALUTE
Italy, Venice (30 July 1979)
Pencil on Fabriano Paper
33.02 cm x 48.26 cm (13 in x 19 in)

EUROPE

TEATRO OLYMPICO - 01
Italy, Vicenza (Undated)
Pen and Ink Drawing with Watercolor Wash on Fabriano Paper
33.02 cm x 48.26 cm (13 in x 19 in)

THE PARADOX OF PLACE: IN THE LINE OF SIGHT

TEATRO OLYMPICO - 02
Italy, Vicenza (Undated)
Pen and Ink Drawing on Fabriano Paper
33.02 cm x 48.26 cm (13 in x 19 in)

EUROPE

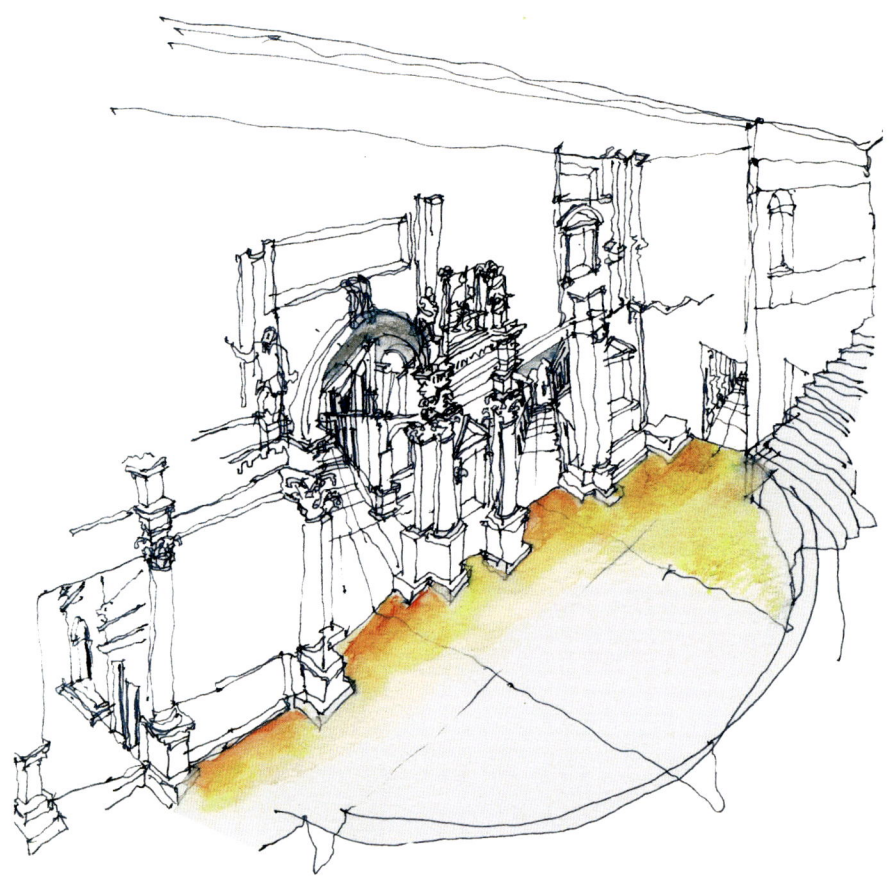

TEATRO OLYMPICO - 03
Italy, Vicenza (Undated)
Pen and Ink Drawing with Watercolor Wash on Fabriano Paper
33.02 cm x 48.26 cm (13 in x 19 in)

THE PARADOX OF PLACE: IN THE LINE OF SIGHT

PIAZZA DUCALE - 01
Italy, Vigevano (October 2001)
Pen and Ink Drawing on Fabriano Paper
33.02 cm x 48.26 cm (13 in x 19 in)

EUROPE

PIAZZA DUCALE - 02
Italy, Vigevano (Undated)
Pen and Ink Drawing on Fabriano Paper
33.02 cm x 48.26 cm (13 in x 19 in)

THE PARADOX OF PLACE: IN THE LINE OF SIGHT

MONTE CARASSO
Switzerland, Monte Carasso (Ticino) (Undated)
Pen and Ink Drawing on Fabriano Paper
33.02 cm x 48.26 cm (13 in x 19 in)

EUROPE

CAMINO TICINESE - 02
Switzerland, Rancate (Ticino) (Undated)
Pen and Ink Drawing with Wash on Fabriano Paper
33.02 cm x 48.26 cm (13 in x 19 in)

THE PARADOX OF PLACE: IN THE LINE OF SIGHT

RIVA SAN VITALE - VIA MO. G.B. MANTEGAZZI
Switzerland, Riva San Vitale (Ticino) (Undated)
Pen and Ink Drawing on Fabriano Paper
33.02 cm x 48.26 cm (13 in x 19 in)

EUROPE

VIA MAROGGIA - 01
Switzerland, Bissone (Ticino) (Undated)
Pen and Ink Drawing on Fabriano Paper
33.02 cm x 48.26 cm (13 in x 19 in)

THE PARADOX OF PLACE: IN THE LINE OF SIGHT

VIA MAROGGIA - 02
Switzerland, Bissone (Ticino) (Undated)
Pen and Ink Drawing on Fabriano Paper
33.02 cm x 48.26 cm (13 in x 19 in)

EUROPE

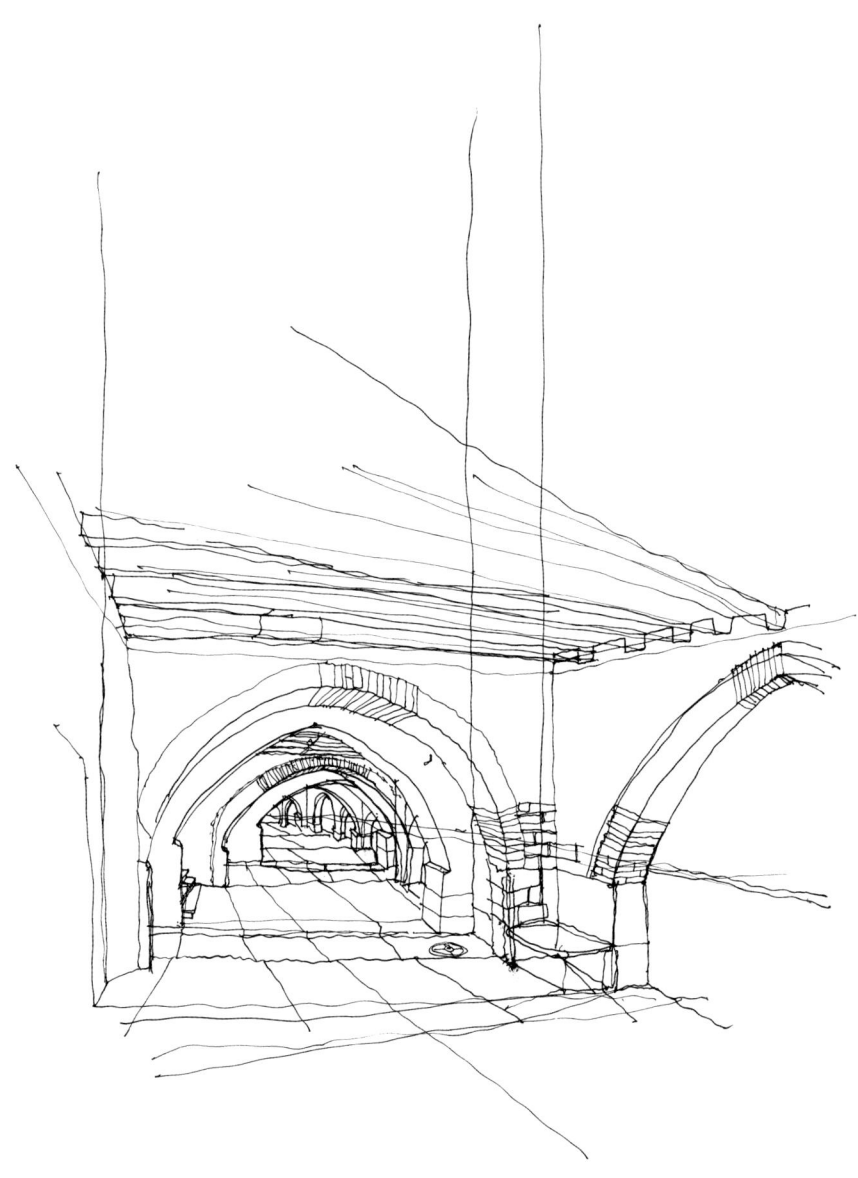

ARCADES
Switzerland, Bissone (Ticino) (Undated)
Pen and Ink Drawing on Fabriano Paper
33.02 cm x 48.26 cm (13 in x 19 in)

THE PARADOX OF PLACE: IN THE LINE OF SIGHT

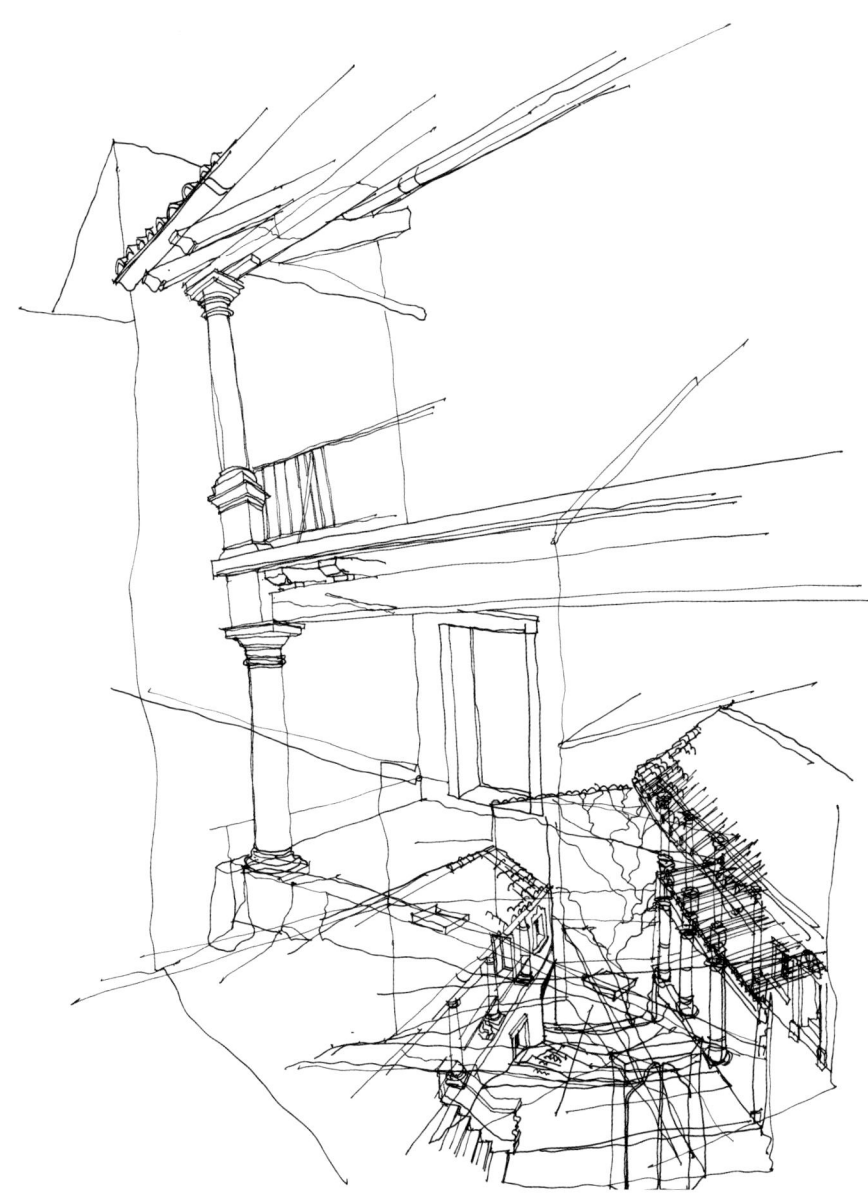

CASA OLDELLI - COURTYARD HOUSE - II
Switzerland, Meride (Ticino) (Undated)
Pen and Ink Drawing on Fabriano Paper
33.02 cm x 48.26 cm (13 in x 19 in)

EUROPE

CASA OLDELLI - COURTYARD HOUSE - III
Switzerland, Meride (Ticino) (Undated)
Pen and Ink Drawing on Fabriano Paper
33.02 cm x 48.26 cm (13 in x 19 in)

CASA OLDELLI - COURTYARD HOUSE - IV
Switzerland, Meride (Ticino) (Undated)
Pen and Ink Drawing on Fabriano Paper
33.02 cm x 48.26 cm (13 in x 19 in)

Steven House + Cathi House

LEARNING TO SEE

Steven House + Cathi House

D. Eugene Egger dedicated his career to inspiring young minds throughout his work as an educator, an architect, a traveler, and an artist. His poetic vision of the world is an inspiration to all of us and an extraordinary gift to the students fortunate enough to travel and learn to see with him. It is this "learning to see" that embodies his core belief as an educator. As Gene says, "Traveling with architecture students for many years has heightened my interest in how one might record the personal confrontation with the "place of a place" to include the monument nestled within. Rapidly advancing digital media, notwithstanding, I have embraced the sketchbook as a visual journal to record and strengthen one's confrontation with vital, visual phenomena, not only the historical precedence of a named place." Drawing is his vehicle to understanding what it is he is seeing – a way of seeing beyond the obvious to something much more profound – to the essence of a place – and capturing that moment of spontaneous awareness, not only on paper, but also within himself.

Gene sees everything about the world as an opportunity to learn, experience, and feel deeply. He views the world around him through the eyes of an architect. He knows that there is no better way to capture a place than to draw it. As he states, "From 'points of view,' hand drawing secures a lasting memory of the place and moments of decisions that structure a scene or an idea. My belief is that a vivid 'storage of memories,' a Herman Hertzberger notion, helps our students of architecture to fully appreciate the manageable complexity of transforming matter and ideas into ordered, habitable environments." His inspiring exhibition takes the viewer on a personal journey throughout the globe and eloquently describes the inspiration and process behind the creation of dozens of his beautiful drawings. Gene Egger has the remarkable ability to delineate, with pen and paper, sketches that are poetic, thoughtful, and captivating. They illustrate a life's work, recording the environment through a few carefully placed lines on paper.

There are many ways of expression, of documenting the world, of developing and sharing a personal vision. Photography, painting, sketching, writing, dancing – each has its use, tools, limits, and possibilities. However, it is the art of the travel sketch that we celebrate in this extraordinary exhibition and publication. Of all the visual mediums, the sketch is perhaps the most challenging – and the most rewarding. A photograph can, perhaps, convey the image more completely – but it can be cluttered with unnecessary distractions and may miss the essence of what the artist was feeling at the moment of the experience. A painting or a drawing may be able to show more through their inherently more complex construction, through color and stroke – but is often a more time-consuming process. A sketch captures the essence of a moment, usually recorded in a short period of time, on a portable, comfortably-sized medium, inviting a certain freedom.

As Gene so eloquently states in describing his process, "Hand drawing is essentially about finding moments contributing to the continuity of a thought or thing. Building these moments into a reconstructed drawing or thing in itself is the primary challenge of visual thinking. My pedagogical efforts over many decades are in making drawings that retain the subject's diversity as well as the subject's iconic presence. Perhaps hand drawing can exhibit a parallel complexity also exhibited by the perceived subject." It is this deeply felt philosophy that explains Gene's inherent desire to document the built environment. And it is through his beautiful drawings that he can share his vision with all of us.

Gene's captivating drawings of Le Corbusier's Chapel at Ronchamp are both fluid and transparent and draw the viewer's eye into and through the building. His sketches capture the spirit and fundamental nature of space while embodying a fluid sense of movement and exploration. As one studies his drawings, one feels almost transported into the building and can feel the essence of the space. It is a rare quality to be able to document places in such a profound way. Gene's dramatic drawing looking over the historic city of Dubrovnik presents a narrow slice of the town below from the top of a steep walkway. His keen sense of perspective provides a detailed three-dimensional depth to the sketch. It gives the viewer the opportunity to see how it feels to experience this beautiful place from high above. In Gene's unique drawing of Café Tomaselli in Salzburg he not only captures the people at the outdoor tables under umbrellas he also includes an adjacent plan to give the viewer a sense of the courtyard's layout.

Making sketch forces one to strip away those extraneous elements and find the spirit of that building or that place, and record that encounter in an intimate, personal way. Sketching is a way of immersing yourself deeply into a moment, and everything about that brief period of time becomes embedded in one's soul. We can look back at sketches made many years ago and remember all the subtleties of that moment – the time of day, the fragrance from the garden, the caress of the breeze, the sound of a dog or children playing. We remember those elements because when you take the time to make a sketch and truly connect with your place, you take that experience into your soul and it becomes a part of you.

We first met Gene as young Virginia Tech architecture students in the fall of 1970 and even at that time we were captivated by his vivid imagination, abounding curiosity, warm spirit and passion for teaching. His mentor, Olivio Ferrari, had invited Gene to Blacksburg to teach in the newly established College of Architecture and this was the perfect place for Gene to flourish. Gene loved to draw, and he strongly encouraged his students to sketch as part of their design process. As close friends of Gene for over 45 years, it has been a joy and an inspiration to watch him and his encounters with his students.

Gene's drawings invite us, to not only journey with him but also to pick up a pen or pencil and join him. The nearly fifty-years of journeys with his students result in the capture of so many intense and profound moments that challenge us to open our eyes and mark the moments of our lives with rich, intimate immersion in our world. Most of us have wished to be an artist at some time in our lives. We stop when we see someone on the street sketching or painting, sensing that they see something we do not, and this pause opens our eyes for a moment to that other world. Some feel as Gene states, "Hand drawing, rather than seen as important visual thinking, is generally considered an outdated, mechanical exercise. A novel ability credited to innate talent." However, his exploratory, engaging drawings invite us all to think, feel, and crave the sensitive awareness and spontaneous expression of making our mark on paper, recording our impressions and understanding, asserting our personalities and vision, and in the process, finding something new within ourselves. Journey well, with joy and passion.

LEARNING TO SEE

GENE EGGER LECTURE - FOUNDATION CLASS
Old High School Building, Blacksburg, VA (1972)
Photograph, Steven + Cathi House

STUDIO REVIEW - FOUNDATION CLASS
Old High School Building, Blacksburg, VA (1972)
Photograph, Steven + Cathi House

147

STORYTELLING
The Lines of Gene Egger

Mitzi Vernon

Monastery – a quintessential Egger site for studying the architecture of community, village or town. In September of 2001, I traveled with Gene Egger on one of his many study abroad ventures, to visit the Certosa di Pavia in Northern Italy. He extracted the monastery on paper as I watched his *practice* – notebook, fountain pen, studio bag, and his thinking hand. We were situated in the arcade, looking out on the grand cloister. If you study the history of the monastery, you imagine the grandness, color and exuberance of the campus, but my memory is steeped in the time of our arrival: the persistent fog and damp of the day and mere weeks after the American tragedy of September 11.

D. EUGENE EGGER AT CERTOSA DI PAVIA
Italy, Pavia (September 2001)
Photograph, Mitzi Vernon

STORYTELLING | The Lines of Gene Egger

Environments at all scales are compositions of short stories of their making and habitation. Time-beaten materials tell tales of how humans and nature leave their mark and how places morph with generations of people, climate, and technology. The Egger sketch is a transparent layering of this history, reminding us that we move *through* space, and that our environments are complex, not composed of isolated objects. Gene speaks often about drawing to *record the encounter*: "When you are traveling you are really often on the outside…you have to imagine going through, around and inside…the strong experience is in *approaching* something. This is part of your perception as well as the thing you finally discover" (http://design.uky.edu/interviews/). He is telling us a story of that site, in a still drawing while capturing his own movement through the place. In his book, *The Thinking Hand*, architect Juhani Pallasmaa describes this phenomenon: "A sketch is in fact a temporal image, a piece of cinematic action recorded as a graphic image." As narrator, Gene models for students their opportunity to author and derive an understanding of the knotty but sublime coming together of material, gravity and passage (of time).

The Certosa di Pavia is a multiple-century story of structure beginning in 1396 and occupied by several orders of monks, including Carthusian, Carmelite, and Cistercian.

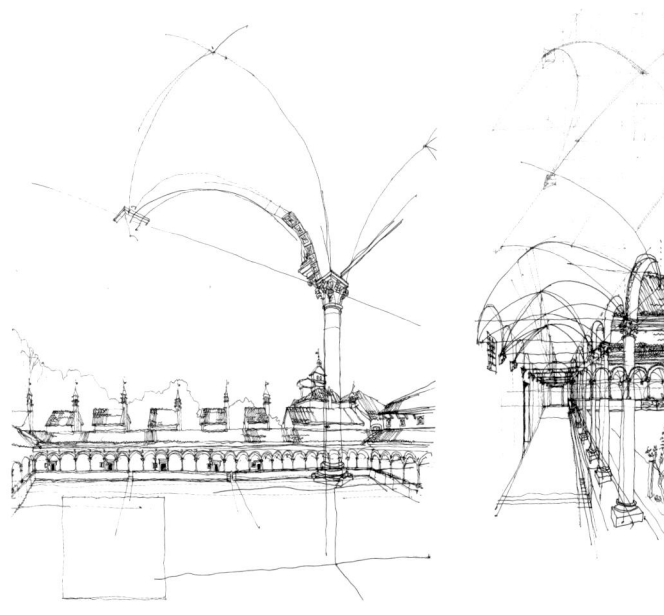

CERTOSA DI PAVIA - 01
Italy, Pavia (September 2001)
Pen and Ink Drawing on Fabriano Paper
33.02 cm x 48.26 cm (13 in x 19 in)

CERTOSA DI PAVIA - 02
Italy, Pavia (September 2001)
Pen and Ink Drawing on Fabriano Paper
33.02 cm x 48.26 cm (13 in x 19 in)

Understanding the structure is about the passage of time, and inherent in that knowledge are the components of the campus architecture, accumulative and executed over centuries. On that day in 2001, I didn't see the church, the portal, the cupola. If not for Gene's drawing I would not have seen the rooftops of the *celle* – the monks' cells. The fog veiled everything for me, except the staccato of columns, the arcade ceiling above and Gene's hands. The gray of the day formed a somber memory, but it is also useful to illustrate that we interpret space through the complicated frame where we stand (physically and psychologically). Fog was both demarcation and disposition.

Gene draws a place as if passing through solid matter allowing us to understand the composition of the building, the town square and the village. Look to any of his sketches for a range of scale handled nimbly by a lofting delicate line suggesting interior or exterior height while abutting the smallest tactile detail, all as if the fingers were tracing the surface of the actual structure. Gene is a master of the juxtaposition of foreground, background and the ground in-between as storytelling.

Writer and editor Tom Jenks discusses the difference between visual and written narration as the difference between expository (e.g., in film), which expounds with "information about characters and story rather than directly **embodying** them" (Jenks, *A Poetics of Fiction*). Ursula K. Le Guin explains story as something that must move but does not necessarily require plot or relentless action; it is often just a **situation**, an unspoken thought or a conversation (Le Guin, *Steering the Craft*). And John Gardner describes "seeing" through words, not as an essayist but by providing imagery for our senses, "…preferably all of them, not just the visual sense – so that we seem to **move among the characters**, **lean with them against the fictional walls**, taste the fictional gazpacho, smell the fictional hyacinths" (Gardner, *The Art of Fiction*). This is Gene's deftness, what separates his architectural hand from others. He draws transparently to explain a situation, exposing detail that we would not otherwise see – storytelling.

"A white-haired man is sitting on a plain wooden bench at a plain wooden table – three boards nailed to four legs – in a small boathouse. The window is open to a view across the water. White is typing on a manual typewriter, and the only other objects are an ashtray and a nail keg," wrote the late William Zinsser about a famous photograph of E. B. White (Zinsser, *On Writing Well*). "The keg, I don't have to be told, is his wastebasket."

The architectural sketch should explain place so well. More importantly perhaps is the reason Zinsser kept the photograph in his Manhattan office: "White has everything he needs." Zinsser explains how tools change, disappear, are replaced, but not the writer. Technology does not make the writer better, rewriting does. We are entrenched in the digital era where analog craft fights for relevance, but tools are only tools. Marvel in their utility, exploit them, but beware of their cunning ability to fool us with a handsome superficial layer and rapid articulation. It is the journey of exploration that is paramount for students, however long and riddled with failure that may be. We should be agile enough to move from one tool to another, fusing them as needed and reserving judgment of the tool's worth. Think as E. B. White – how little do I need to make and remake?

The thing about that E. B. White photograph hanging in Zinsser's office…so many students saw it. Gene Egger traveled abroad once or twice a year for over 30 years, taking along more than 1,500 students during that span. Lucky them.

D. EUGENE EGGER AT CERTOSA DI PAVIA
Italy, Pavia (September 2001)
Photograph, Mitzi Vernon

Paul Emmons

NEVER A DAY WITHOUT A LINE
TRAVELING SKETCHBOOKS AND THE EDUCATION OF ARCHITECTS

Paul Emmons

So said the great ancient Greek painter Apelles, according to Pliny, emphasizing the need to practice drawing daily.[1] This advice is especially true for the itinerant architect – never a day without a sketch. Leonardo da Vinci was one of many inspired by Apelles' famous maxim and incessantly filled his sketchbooks with drawings (even on saints' feast days when one was not to work), counseling artists to "go about and constantly as you go observe and consider. …And take a note with slight strokes in a little book which you should always carry with you."[2]

Before the modern era, acquiring drawing skills was an important part of any person's education because that was the only way to record things seen.[3] Architects' drawings were especially cherished and bequeathed in wills to the next generation.[4] Architects copied others' sketchbook images into their own sketchbooks, presumably when they met in a common city. Images in antiquarian Ciriaco d'Ancona's (1391-1452) sketchbook from his travels in Athens and Constantinople – places very difficult to get to from western Europe at the time – were copied by many architects into their own sketchbooks, including that of architect Giuliano da Sangallo.[5] During the Renaissance, there was a "lively tradition of exchange, in which drawings circulated among many architects and each created their own variations.[6]" In this way, images provide their own travelogue.

Architects' use of sketchbooks for study during travel is a very old practice, preceding even the availability of paper in the west. During the thirteenth-century, Frenchman Villard de Honnecourt filled more than forty sheets of parchment made from animal skin with figures and buildings that he saw during his travels around Europe. Since parchment was very expensive in the Middle Ages, Villard's sketchbook was of poor quality with occasional holes; it's leaves were often scraped of ink and reused many times creating layered linear palimpsests. The roughly 7x10 inch book has a soft cover that folds over the leaves and can be tied to protect it in his cloak while riding on horseback.[7] With the many different kinds of papers and drawing media available today, architects strive to find just the right match when wedding pencil to paper.

There has been a close relationship between design education and travel embedded in architecture culture for centuries.[8] Travel, deriving from the French travail, was synonymous with painful labor, struggle, and suffering.[9] In the sixteenth century, when Sir Philip Sydney was giving his brother advice for travel on the continent, he told him to "carry a notebook and a red crayon" but also to "never journey without something to eat in your pocket, if only to throw to dogs when attacked by them."[10] The Grand Tour usually extended over several years and was limited to the wealthy elite.

Learning through sketching while traveling was extremely difficult for most architects until the nineteenth century and the beginnings of mass tourism. Thomas Cook, the creator of the first travel agency and based in London, hosted its first continental tour in 1855.[11] In 1894, the American Academy in Rome was established to send its own Rome Prize fellows to the Eternal City. With the relative ease of travel in the jet age, travel study trips became part of an architect's basic training by the second half of the twentieth century.[12]

Today, educational travel has become difficult to distinguish from mass-market tourism. The first portable camera made by Kodak became available in 1888. The camera, now the phone camera, reigns supreme over touristic vision. While photography can be an extremely expressive art, tourists' photos usually aim no higher than to reproduce well-known postcard views as selfies. Important sites worthy of visiting are authenticated through endless reproductions.[13]

Even in today's immersive electronic access to any image anywhere, why do architects still pursue travel with sketchbooks in hand? Unlike most fields that turn inward, the architect's research laboratories are the great cities all around the world. To know a place, designers must be bodily immersed in its culture, its cuisine, and its stones because architecture is multi-sensorial. Sketchbooks manifest the difference between educational travel for architects and mass tourism. While photos are fast, drawings are slow. We "take" photos, but "make" sketches. Snapping a photo has become a substitute for looking. Sketching demands extended observation. The sort of looking that occurs through drawing results in revealing something not seen before. The experience of buildings, cities and landscapes can only be fully tasted and chewed in their slow immediacy.

For the peripatetic student, a sketchbook is ready at hand and ever present. At the voyage's outset, the pages of the prescient sketchbook are empty but full of optimistic potential. As the trip unfolds, the pages slowly fill with memories. It tends to fill from beginning to end, though as with memories, earlier work may be revisited again and again in the cool calm of the evening. Like anthropologists' field notebooks, sketchbooks are also diaries of events recording the daily mundane alongside occasional profound insights. Bits of paper – a ticket stub, a museum postcard, a napkin doodle – collected along the way are often collaged and interleaved into the sketchbook's pages.[14]

While we think of architectural drawings as dealing primarily with space, it is their temporality that distinguishes sketches. Among different sorts of drawings, the sketch is the most rapid. The status of the sketchbook is lowest in the fine arts, the least refined and unpretentious. However, it is also closest to the immediacy of artistic creation, of insight. Drawing for architects is not to record preformed ideas; it is to create them within the act of drawing. Accidental drips of coffee or wine challenge the drafter to integrate them into an unfinished drawing. Sketches capture the gesture of the hand, the pulse of the blood and the breath of the drafter. The frozen gesture of a pen line tells us if it was made hurriedly, lovingly or searchingly.

While the compound word "sketchbook" is relatively recent, sketch comes from Italian *schizzo*, which in turn derives from a Greek word *schedios* meaning done or made off-hand, extempore.[15] (Ex)-tempore is (out of)-time and tells us that the sketch participates in a special temporal condition known as *festina lente*; the fast/slow action of looking and drawing that connects the drafter to the place. One must look a long time in order to be able to draw rapidly. When Viennese architect Camillo Sitte first visited a city, he began by ascending a tower to have an overview, then he dined at the finest restaurant in the main public square, and only afterwards began to make sketches.[16]

Improvisational drawing while traveling uniquely aids architects to discover the new in the old. During Le Corbusier's 1911 trip to Rome, he saw the eternal city, but through his sketching, he discovered a new modern architecture of pure form.[17] During Louis Kahn's 1951 trip through Egypt and Greece, he saw ancient architectural monuments, but through his sketching, he discovered in them a new modern architecture of mass and light.[18] The best sketches not only record what is visible, they peer beyond into the invisible.

NOTES

[1] Pliny, *Natural History*, 35.84. Quoted and discussed in Sarah Blacke McHam, *Pliny and the Artistic Culture of the Italian Renaissance* (New Haven: Yale University Press, 2013) 85.

[2] Leonardo, *Codex Urbinas*, 38v-39r (McMahon, Treatise, I, 53, para. 80) cited in McHam, p. 166.

[3] Varro, Will of John Symonds, Appendix 1 in John Summerson 'Three Elizabethan Architects' *Bulletin of the John Rylands Library* 40 (1957-58) 202-228, 223.

[4] Beverly Brown and Diana Kleiner, "Giuliano da Sangallo's Drawings after Ciriaco d'Ancona: Transformations of Greek and Roman Antiquities in Athens" *Journal of the Society of Architectural Historians* Vol. 42, No. 4 (Dec., 1983), 321-335.

[5] Cammy Brothers, "Drawing in the Void: The Space between the Sketchbook and the Treatise" in *Some degree of happiness, Studi di storia dell'architettura in onore di Howard Burns*, edited by Maria Beltramini and Caroline Elam (Pisa: Scuola Normale, 2010) pp. 93-105, 667-680, 105.

[6] Carl Barnes, Jr., *The Portfolio of Villard de Honnecourt* (Ashgate: 2009) 2-5.

[7] Denise Costanzo, "Travel, Trips, Study Abroad: Instructive Displacements" in *Architecture School*, eds. Joan Ockman and Rebecca Williamson (MIT Press, 2012) 402-408, 402.

[8] "Travel, n." OED Online. Oxford University Press, December 2016. Web. 20 January 2017.

[9] Ernest Stuart Bates, *Touring in 1600: A Study in the Development of Travel as a Means of Education* (Houghton Mifflin, 1912) 59.

[10] https://www.thomascook.com/thomas-cook-history/. Accessed Jan 29, 2017.

[11] Denise Costanzo, "Travel, Trips, Study Abroad: Instructive Displacements" in *Architecture School*, eds. Joan Ockman and Rebecca Williamson (MIT Press, 2012) 402-408, 402, 405.

[12] Chuck Stephen, "The Search for Authenticity: Review Essay of Dean MacCannell, The Tourist" *Berkeley Journal of Sociology*, Vol. 35 (1990), pp. 151-156. Emily Greenwald, "On the History of Photography and Site/Sight Seeing at Yellowstone" *Environmental History* Vol. 12, No. 3 (Jul., 2007), pp. 654-660.

[13] Sightseeing is an 'extensive ceremonial agenda.' Erving Goffman, *Relations in Public* (New York: Harper and Row, 1971) 63.

[14] Gandy glued in additional pages into a sketchbook he took with him on a northern trip. Ian Goodall and Margaret Richardson, "A Recently Discovered Gandy Sketchbook" *Architectural History*, Vol. 44, Essays in Architectural History Presented to John Newman (2001) 45-56.

[15] "Sketch, n." OED Online. Oxford University Press, December 2016. Web. 20 January 2017. The earliest use of the word sketch-book recorded in OED is from 1820. "Sketch-book, n." OED Online. Oxford University Press, December 2016. Web. 20 January 2017.

[16] George Collins and Christiane Craseman Collins, *Camillo Sitte and the Birth of Modern City Planning* (Rizzoli, 1986) 63, quoted in Marcia Feuerstein, "Camillo Sitte's winged snail: *Festina lente* and escargot" in *Confabulations, Storytelling in Architecture*, Paul Emmons, Marcia Feuerstein and Carolina Dayer, eds. (Routledge, 2017) 137.

[17] Le Corbusier, *Creation is a Patient Search*, transl. James Palmes (NY: Praeger, 1960) 37.

[18] Jan Hochstim, *The Paintings and Sketches of Louis I. Kahn* (New York: Rizzoli, 1991).

Mark A. Blizard

FIELD STUDIES

Mark A. Blizard

IN RETROSPECT, IT MAY SEEM OBVIOUS: ALL TRUE JOURNEYS BEGIN FROM THE SAME PORT. Indeed, I carry certain places and certain teachers with me – although they often seem indistinct. Appearing as vague recollections or fragmentary images, they still, at a profound level, shape my gestures and thoughts. The design laboratory at Virginia Tech as taught by Professor Egger has remained cogent, retaining its coherence and over time, becoming even more vital in my own practice and teaching. Each semester as I set out once again, I draw from a vast catalog of experiences, images and examples. They remain potent though uncertain and never definitive: as I look closely, passing them back and forth in my mind, I continue to make discoveries. Discussions on architecture or education always seem to return to those early laboratories whose form was structured on the unspoken pedagogy of the sketchbook. The sketchbook became the site of architectural inquiry, a means of gathering images and ideas and a lens to focus and refine thought. I recall Professor Egger, in a lecture several years after those first foundation laboratories, stressing that design was a dialectic practice whose center is the slow observation and inquiry into the *presence of a place*. The first instrument of practice is observation. For Egger, the chosen media for this encounter are the sketchbook and the pen. As with all instruments, these conjointly take measure of the habitable environment and transform our perception of it. The sketchbook is a mode of probing, of seeing the "horizon of meanings" beyond and beneath the surface appearance of things.[1] And in so doing, each sketch also explores the complex nature of our experience.

The city is more than an incidental setting for Egger's practice; it is the central source. In wandering through the streets of an unfamiliar city or returning again to the slowly decaying towns of western Virginia, he discovers fundamental questions about architectural presence, design, and education. Each sketch offers a new perspective and an opportunity to grasp, with a little more lucidity, some rare or fleeting thought. The fabric of artifacts and spaces that form the deep tissue of material culture face him with *the accumulated density of a history*.[2] The city becomes a laboratory and a teacher where we search for worthy questions, where connections are made between unlikely or seemingly dissimilar things, where techniques become gestures and gestures become thoughts. We gain our footing as we search for the very roots of things. For Egger as an architect, the sketchbook is the portmanteau that gathers the city in fragments of experience and thought in the attempt to make sense of each encounter with a place.[3]

I recall a series of photographs that Egger took with the camera mounted above his dining room table. Over the course of several weeks, dozens of photographs documented each change of the table landscape. First, we see the table as the site for a romantic dinner, and later, a family gathering; it is then transformed into a desk for homework or for bill-paying. Along the way, through each of these changes and the enumerable elements that accompanied each different use, the table remains remarkably stable – like a small city. The city, or any landscape for that matter, is not a body of static objects and our experience of it is not linear and sequential, but as a dense field of agencies, enjambments, contaminations, and overlays. Other than when they are contained in museums or books, things are always perceived as inseparable from their context. The city is no different. The strata of each sketch are corollaries to the facets of our experience of the space of the city. The city is perceived in these sketches as an active field that expands and contracts, enveloping us. But it is also a structure whose persistence lends stability to the continual flux of time and event. Le Corbusier proposed that it was this architectural promenade that allows us to make sense of architectural space. First, we move one way and then another; glancing, turning, "the forms take on meaning, they expand, they combine with one another […] We walk, we turn, we never stop moving or turning towards things."[4] Egger's sketches are field studies, composed at a series of pauses within the procession. Positions and views that are carefully selected at moments where place is at its most evident.

The correspondence that Egger finds between place and the sketch involves sorting each place out, passing it back and forth in his mind, deforming it slightly, and focusing on what is essential or at least particular – giving the place its identity or character. His sketches do not seek to arrive at some final goal or attempt to contain a faithful transcription of the actual world, but one that is shaped by the limitations, characteristics, and possibilities inherent in the media and the process, in drawing techniques, and in the imagination of the architect. To draw a line is to at once conceive of the line, which is to say, to imagine its presence. The sketch focuses and directs our thinking, like a map that only presents certain aspects of a territory and is guided by discernment and the ability to discriminate between what is the focus or purpose of the work and what is to be passed over.

Mark A. Blizard

Sketching is a slow and repetitive process of sorting through and discerning a clear and cogent utterance from out of a background that is dense with static and superfluous detail. Clearly, that which is not drawn is as important as the lines that are. Over the course of time, Egger has learned what to leave out. At some point, each sketch must be abandoned, incomplete, inchoate and still open to interpretation or imagination.

Every sketch is both local and universal. Each reflects the immediacy of a particular encounter. Through this encounter, a fine mesh is woven that captures the resistance of matter as it traces out lines of thought. The objects of material culture – when studied long enough, or under certain conditions of light, or following a long absence, or when he chooses to see them as unfamiliar – reveal or reflect something akin to ideas themselves. Looking upon these fragmentary encounters, contours of places and events appear. Sketching, like the collage of layers of unlikely fragments, slows him down to where he absorbs the many facets of the moment.

If his field studies can be described as dialogs with the city, they also can be understood as in dialog with books and ideas. A few examples will have to suffice. The sketch of the towers and streets of San Gimignano can be understood as a cognitive map.

SAN GIMIGNANO
Italy, San Gimignano (Undated)
Pen and Ink Drawing on Fabriano Paper
33.02 cm x 48.26 cm (13 in x 19 in)

CAMPO PASSAGE VICOLO DEL VANNELLO
Italy, Siena (13 November 1991)
Pen and Ink Drawing on Fabriano Paper
33.02 cm x 48.26 cm (13 in x 19 in)

FIELD STUDIES

In conversation with Kevin Lynch, specifically his book *The Image of the City*, Egger explores the city as a body of typical and repeating elements that form legible patterns and images.

In his dense sketch of the passages between the Campo and Via di Citta in Siena, we read a dialog with Gordon Cullen and Ivor de Wolfe who understood the visual coherence and spatial organization of the European townscape through the phenomena of serial vision and the contrast between sequential visual frames.

In his habit of walking in the city, we can see a distinct reference to Michel de Certeau's book, *The Practice of Everyday Life*. Through sketching, the city emerges as an "ensemble of possibilities and interdictions" which are actualized through a practice of sketching akin to improvisation. De Certeau's walker, like the sketcher, "transforms each spatial signifier into something else."[5]

Merleau-Ponty's *Phenomenology of Perception* seems present as a foundation for much of Egger's thinking. Egger perceives the encounter as an embodied perception that forms a dialectic of milieu and action. Each maneuver, each line or mark in the sketchbook, "modifies the character of the field and establishes in it new lines of force." Through this dialectic, the sketch unfolds.[6]

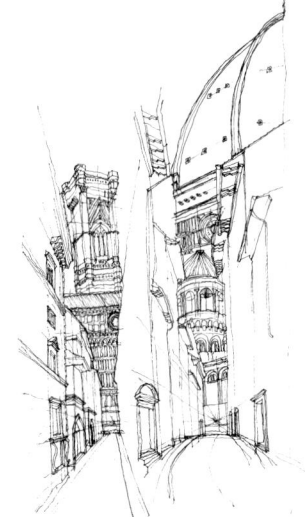

GRAVE HILL CHURCH
United States, Virginia, Simmonsville (Undated)
Pen and Ink Drawing on Fabriano Paper
33.02 cm x 48.26 cm (13 in x 19 in)

FIRENZA - DUOMO VIEW VIA DEL STUDIO - 01
Italy, Florence (Undated)
Pen and Ink Drawing on Fabriano Paper
33.02 cm x 48.26 cm (13 in x 19 in)

Egger's sketch of the Gravel Hill Church in Simmonsville, Virginia seems to parallel Giancarlo de Carlo's heuristic process of reading the territory. This sketch is an inquiry into the site, the use of materials, and the repetition of fundamental architectural elements. Together, these combine to form a logic binding earth and the inhabitable space of cultural forms. Examined as a whole rather than as a series of discrete autonomous images or elements, place is understood by its architectural presence – what De Carlo calls its genetic code.[7]

The sketch of the Duomo in Florence can be read as part of an open dialog with Henri Lefebvre about the representation of space as it "combines the city's reality with its ideality, embracing the practical, the symbolic and the imaginary."[8] The campanile and the Duomo are encountered as impositions set defiantly into the urban fabric and as inseparable from that fabric: the ideals of Renaissance humanism are inextricable from the space, texture, and history of the city.

Underneath each encounter and each dialog, we are left with the sketches themselves. In them, Egger returns again and again to the intensely local and concrete as if it holds a code that can be interpreted.[9] Within the space of a single sketch, his inquiry shifts its focus from armatures to elements, from landscape and vista to perspective and sequential movement along a street, to a small detail – such as a spigot – that would otherwise be overlooked. Within the course of a single line that is drawn across the whiteness of the page, surfaces take on the solidity of mass, becoming walls, only to lose their weight, becoming transparent, almost ephemeral. Between elements, details and joints make their appearance. His lines are articulated at their beginnings and endings and where they join. These serve to stitch the gestures of each hand movement together and at the same time, to anchor the sketch to the page. And even this single line is composed of infinitesimally small movements that cannot be separated or even distinguished. The lines themselves are not clear and autonomous things but are better understood as a language of thinking and seeing, of considering space and distance and the weight of matter. After consideration, when all of this is set aside, what we find is a collection of compelling sketches whose mystery remains unabated and undiminished.

FIELD STUDIES

NOTES

[1] Lefebvre, H. (1991). *The Production of Space*. Malden, MAs: Blackwell Printing. p222.
[2] Barrett, W. (1979). *The Illusion of Technique*. New York: Anchor Books. p44.
[3] I believe that Egger looks upon these sketches as encounters with what the anthropologist Clifford Geertz refers to as "densely mediated webs of significance." Rather than a linear series of isolated images, I find enmeshed in these sketches, the depth of each experience: thought, memory, certain tastes and smells, essences, emotions and moods—are revealed. In turn, they intermingle with time and history. It is as if each sketch contains an entire narrative, or a morality play, or contains some semblance of the origin of built form. Sketching for Egger is similar to what Geertz terms a "thick description" of place in that observation, recording, and analysis are not autonomous processes. See: Clifford Geertz. 1973. *The Interpretation of Cultures*. New York: Basic Books. pp5–6, 20.
[4] Le Corbusier as cited by Daniele Pauly. 2008. *Le Corbusier: The Chapel at Ronchamp*. Basel: Birkhäuser. p29.
[5] de Certeau, M. (1988). *The Practice of Everyday Life*. Los Angeles: University of California Press. p98.
[6] Ponty, M. (2016). *Phenomenology of Perception* as referenced by Alberto Perez-Gomez. *Attunement: Architectural Meaning after the Crisis of Modern Science*. Cambridge, Massachusetts: MIT Press. p144.
[7] See: McKean, J. (2004). *Giancarlo de Carlo: Layered Places*. London: Edition Axel Menges. pp48–51.
[8] Lefebvre, p74.
[9] "All meanings are born within the human world of the everyday." Barrett, p74.

Michael OBrien

LEARNING BY OBSERVING

Michael OBrien

I'VE BEEN READING ERIC R. KANDEL'S *REDUCTIONISM IN ART AND BRAIN SCIENCE* for the last few flight hours and thinking about Professor Gene Egger. I was never formally a student of his, but I did learn from him by observing the annual exhibition of student work that documented their travel experience. The exhibitions frequently included photographs, but always contained drawings. The sketchbooks themselves would be exhibited, with pages including notations, diagrams, watercolors, ticket stubs, all clear signs they had documented their trip. I also hear the voice of Professor Olivio Ferrari stating "What's the idee? What did you learn?"

    The drawings from Professor Egger's students were different from the picturesque sketches I had grown accustomed to seeing at other architecture schools. These images were both beautiful and accurate mimics of a camera; but again, I thought "What did you learn?" Through thoughtful reflection, I contend that the difference in these representations rests in the conceptual framework that guided their creation. These drawings were constructions with precise and layered information and used light as an armature upon which students carefully discovered, recorded, and annotated spatial proportions. Many times, these embodiments of place included a floor plan or section beneath the perspective. While somewhat puzzling at first glance, I quickly realized that it was also the best way to understand the architect's rules and guiding principles and demonstrate that what worked on the facade by way of regulation and proportion likewise worked as a control for the plan and section. It struck me that by teaching the students to study what lay beneath the facade, Professor Egger was showing them how to listen to architects who preceded them by decades or hundreds of years. It was clear that history was no longer about memorizing styles and dates; rather, history was an active device for communicating between the past to the present through the pen nibs of the students and by extension, a direct connection to their future work.

    Since drafting these paragraphs, I had the fortunate opportunity to lead a study abroad experience and travel with my students to Italy. I've watched the students develop their drawings from simple shapes and textures to portrayals that present emotions, complex spatial organizations, and urban conditions. My personal sketches also recorded the challenges of structuring multifaceted surfaces and volumes (mostly unsuccessfully) while capturing urban elements and street spaces. But the "Why draw?" question coming from the students was always in my mind. Formal structures aside, I believe that by simply investing time in a drawing and by making an effort to look closely, of being slow, adjusting to error, will form an embedded image of our time together in these Italian venues. Of course, there are also approximately ten thousand searchable digital photographs that will accompany the hundreds of sketches and drawings that more closely link to my consciousness than these photographs.

  I remember choosing Virginia Tech for my graduate studies because it was the only school I visited that I didn't understand. Faculty like Regan, Ferrari, Brown, Daniel, the Dunays, and Gene Egger had constructed a scaffolded pedagogy that began with the complex geometric underpinnings of space and form. When these fundamentals bonded to the school's rigorous travel program, the studio lessons transformed from stylistic outcomes into architectural propositions that enabled the students to compete in today's global practice. Similar to my desires to join Professor Egger in Europe, I wish I had been able to attend his exhibition and workshop in Lexington and his walkabout through Kentucky; however, I look forward to this publication of his constructed drawings, to learn in the same way that I did year's earlier.

PIAZZA DELLA REPUBBLICA (CORTONA)
Italy, Cortona (18 April 2018)
Pen and Ink Drawing with Watercolor Wash on Fabriano Paper; Image Michael OBrien
6.35 cm x 9.525 cm (2.5 in x 3.75 in)

NORTH AMERICA

CENTRAL AMERICA

SANTO TOMAS - SUNDAY MARKET
Guatamala, Chichicastenango (18 March 1979)
Pen and Ink Drawing on Fabriano Paper
33.02 cm x 48.26 cm (13 in x 19 in)

THE PARADOX OF PLACE: IN THE LINE OF SIGHT

FLIGHT WAIT - AVIATECA TO TIKAL
Guatamala, Guatamala City (14 March 1979)
Pen and Ink Drawing with Wash on Fabriano Paper
33.02 cm x 48.26 cm (13 in x 19 in)

UNITED STATES

FIVE POINTS
United States, Virginia, Five Points (Undated)
Pen and Ink Drawing on Fabriano Paper
33.02 cm x 48.26 cm (13 in x 19 in)

THE PARADOX OF PLACE: IN THE LINE OF SIGHT

RTE. 42 BETHEL METHODIST TWIN CHURCHES
United States, Virginia, Craig County (Fall 1995)
Pen and Ink Drawing on Fabriano Paper
33.02 cm x 48.26 cm (13 in x 19 in)

UNITED STATES

APPROACH FROM OLD TOWN ROAD
United States, Virginia, Shawsville (Undated)
Pen and Ink Drawing on Fabriano Paper
33.02 cm x 48.26 cm (13 in x 19 in)

THE PARADOX OF PLACE: IN THE LINE OF SIGHT

FROM N-S TRACKS
United States, Virginia, Shawsville (Undated)
Pen and Ink Drawing on Fabriano Paper
33.02 cm x 48.26 cm (13 in x 19 in)

UNITED STATES

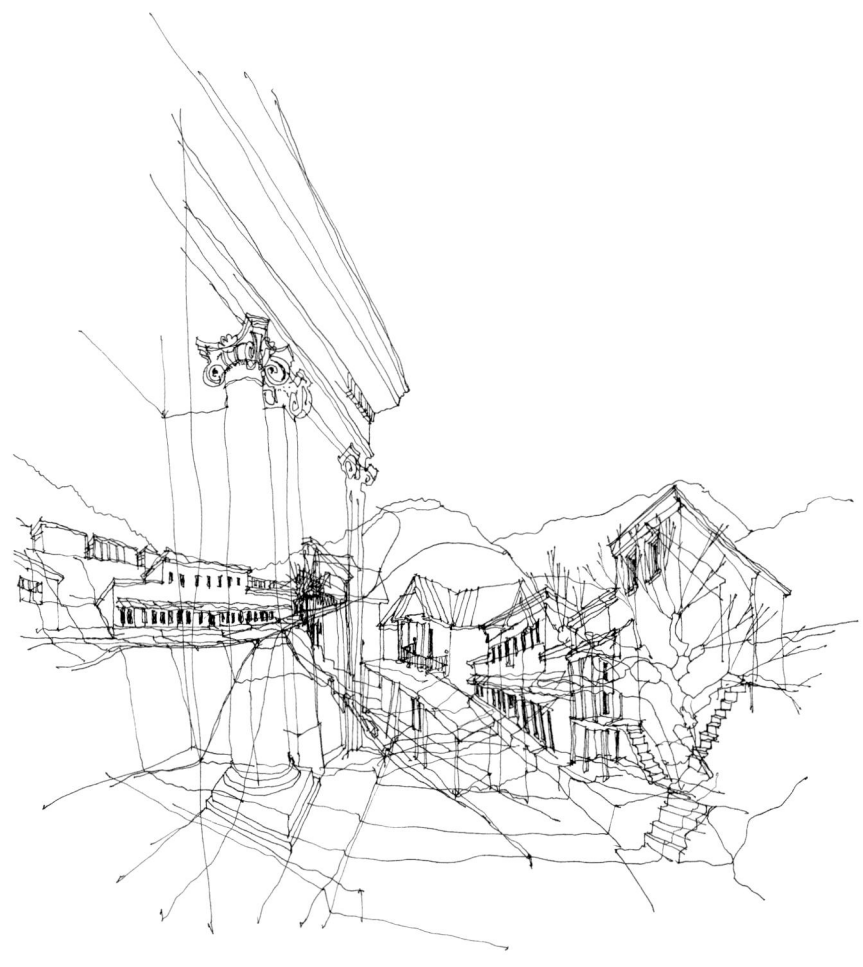

OLD TOWN ROAD
United States, Virginia, Shawsville (Undated)
Pen and Ink Drawing on Fabriano Paper
33.02 cm x 48.26 cm (13 in x 19 in)

THE PARADOX OF PLACE: IN THE LINE OF SIGHT

RTE. 42 FROM GRAVEL HILL
United States, Virginia, Simmonsville (Undated)
Pen and Ink Drawing on Fabriano Paper
33.02 cm x 48.26 cm (13 in x 19 in)

UNITED STATES

APPROACH FROM RTE. 42
United States, Virginia, Simmonsville (Undated)
Pen and Ink Drawing with Wash on Fabriano Paper
33.02 cm x 48.26 cm (13 in x 19 in)

THE PARADOX OF PLACE: IN THE LINE OF SIGHT

GRAVE HILL CHURCH
United States, Virginia, Simmonsville (Undated)
Pen and Ink Drawing on Fabriano Paper
33.02 cm x 48.26 cm (13 in x 19 in)

UNITED STATES

CHRISTIAN CHURCH
United States, Virginia, Snowville (Undated)
Pen and Ink Drawing on Fabriano Paper
33.02 cm x 48.26 cm (13 in x 19 in)

THE PARADOX OF PLACE: IN THE LINE OF SIGHT

RESIDENCE ROW
United States, Virginia, Snowville (Undated)
Pen and Ink Drawing on Fabriano Paper
33.02 cm x 48.26 cm (13 in x 19 in)

UNITED STATES

EARLY COMPANY TOWNS OF THE VIRGINIAS - CASS AERIAL PHOTOGRAPH
United States, West Virginia, Cass (1982)
Aerial Photograph

THE PARADOX OF PLACE: IN THE LINE OF SIGHT

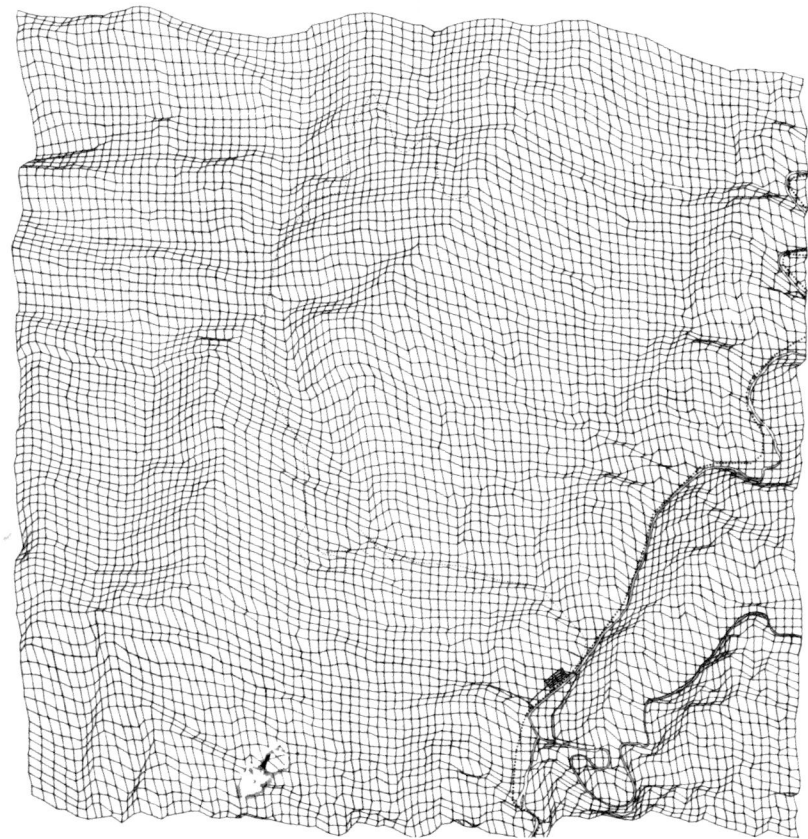

EARLY COMPANY TOWNS OF THE VIRGINIAS - CASS DIGITAL TOPOGRAPHY
United States, West Virginia, Cass (1982)
Digital Drawing

UNITED STATES

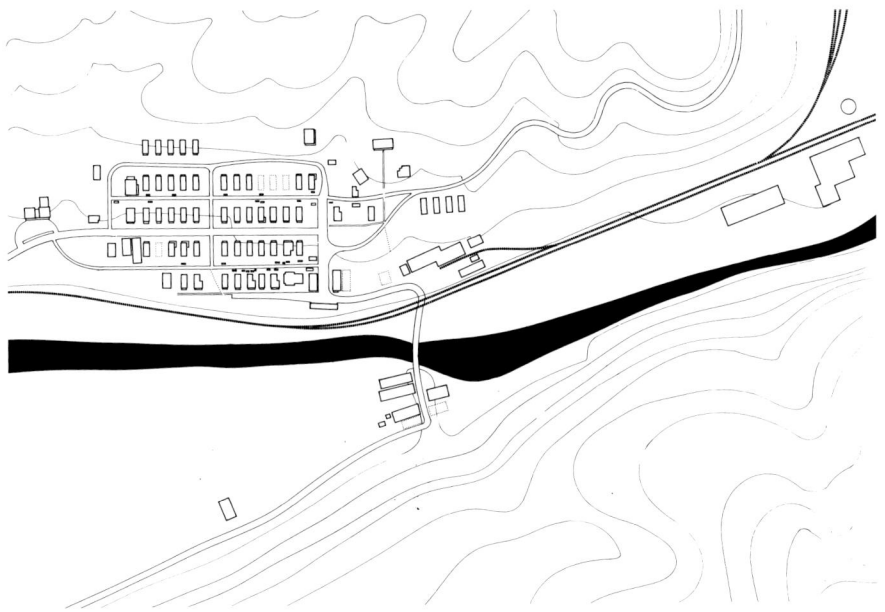

EARLY COMPANY TOWNS OF THE VIRGINIAS - CASS TOWN PLAN
United States, West Virginia, Cass (1982)
Line Drawing

THE PARADOX OF PLACE: IN THE LINE OF SIGHT

EARLY COMPANY TOWNS OF THE VIRGINIAS - CASS ENTRY
United States, West Virginia, Cass (1982)
Pen and Ink Drawing on Fabriano Paper
33.02 cm x 48.26 cm (13 in x 19 in)

UNITED STATES

EARLY COMPANY TOWNS OF THE VIRGINIAS - CASS WORKER HOUSING
United States, West Virginia, Cass (1982)
Pen and Ink Drawing on Fabriano Paper
33.02 cm x 48.26 cm (13 in x 19 in)

THE PARADOX OF PLACE: IN THE LINE OF SIGHT

EARLY COMPANY TOWNS OF THE VIRGINIAS - CASS VIEW FROM ALLEY
United States, West Virginia, Cass (1982)
Pen and Ink Drawing on Fabriano Paper
33.02 cm x 48.26 cm (13 in x 19 in)

UNITED STATES

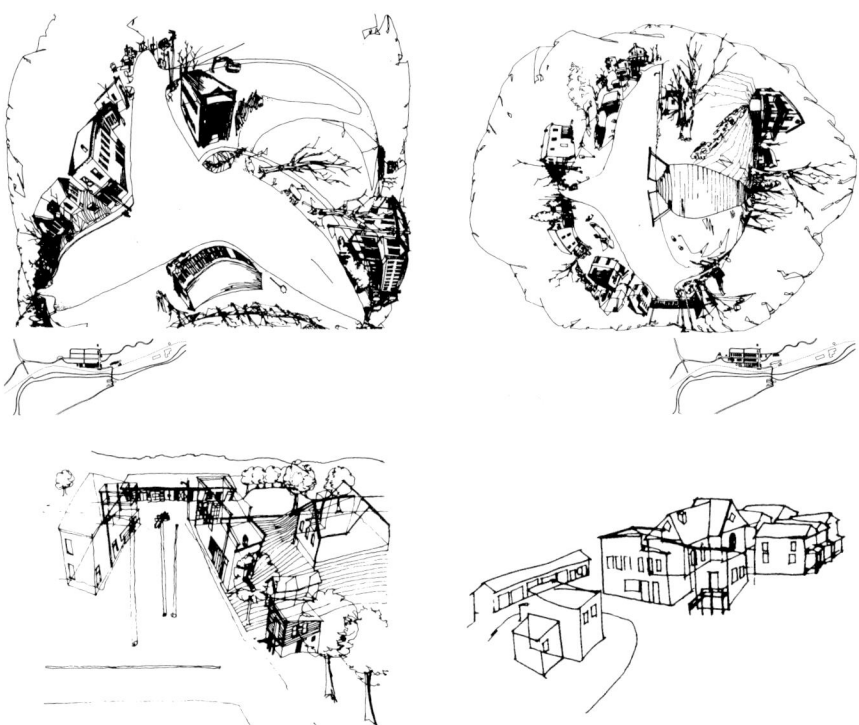

EARLY COMPANY TOWNS OF THE VIRGINIAS - CASS INTERSECTIONS
United States, West Virginia, Cass (1982)
Pen and Ink Drawing on Fabriano Paper
33.02 cm x 48.26 cm (13 in x 19 in)

THE PARADOX OF PLACE: IN THE LINE OF SIGHT

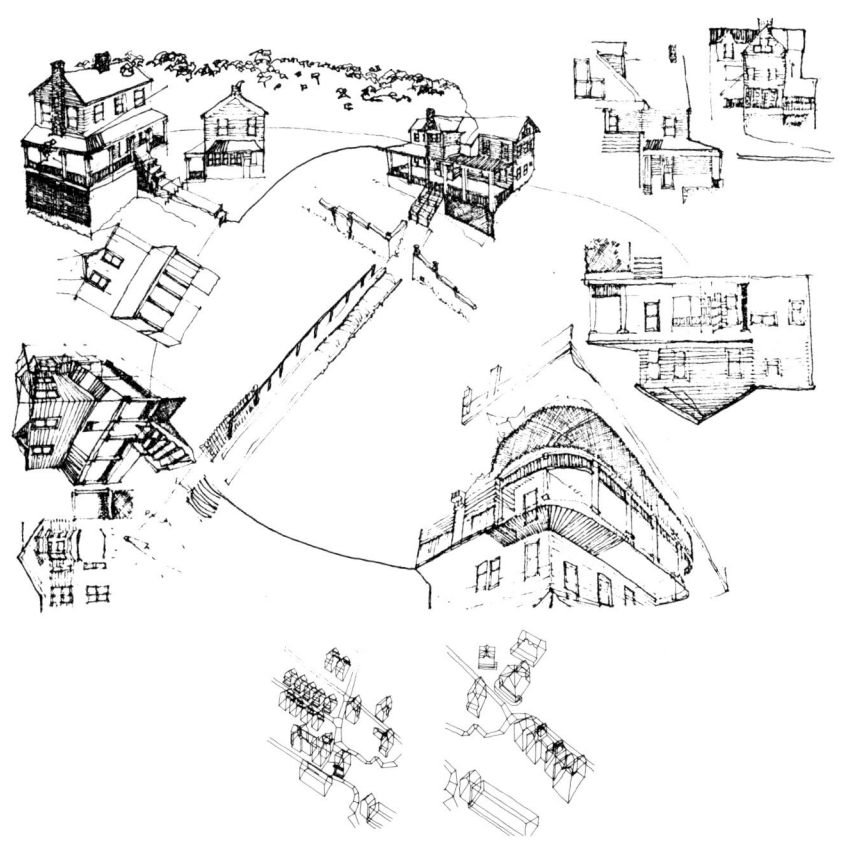

EARLY COMPANY TOWNS OF THE VIRGINIAS - CASS PUBLIC CLUSTERS
United States, West Virginia, Cass (1982)
Pen and Ink Drawing on Fabriano Paper
33.02 cm x 48.26 cm (13 in x 19 in)

UNITED STATES

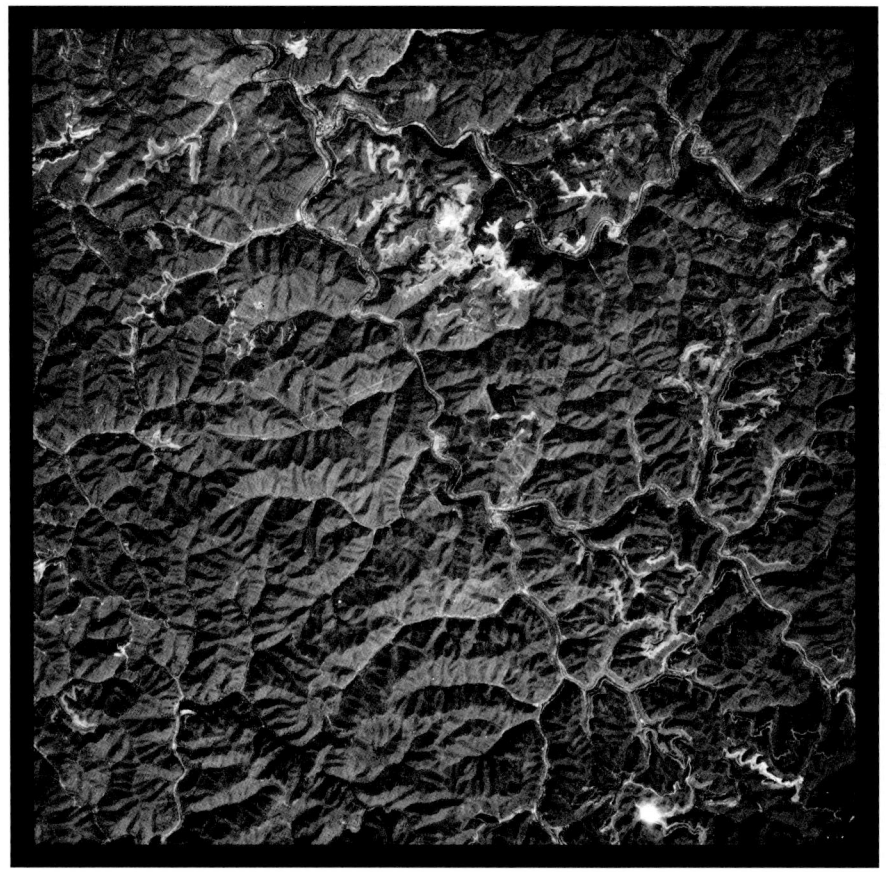

EARLY COMPANY TOWNS OF THE VIRGINIAS - GARY AERIAL PHOTOGRAPH
United States, West Virginia, Gary (1982)
Aerial Photograph

THE PARADOX OF PLACE: IN THE LINE OF SIGHT

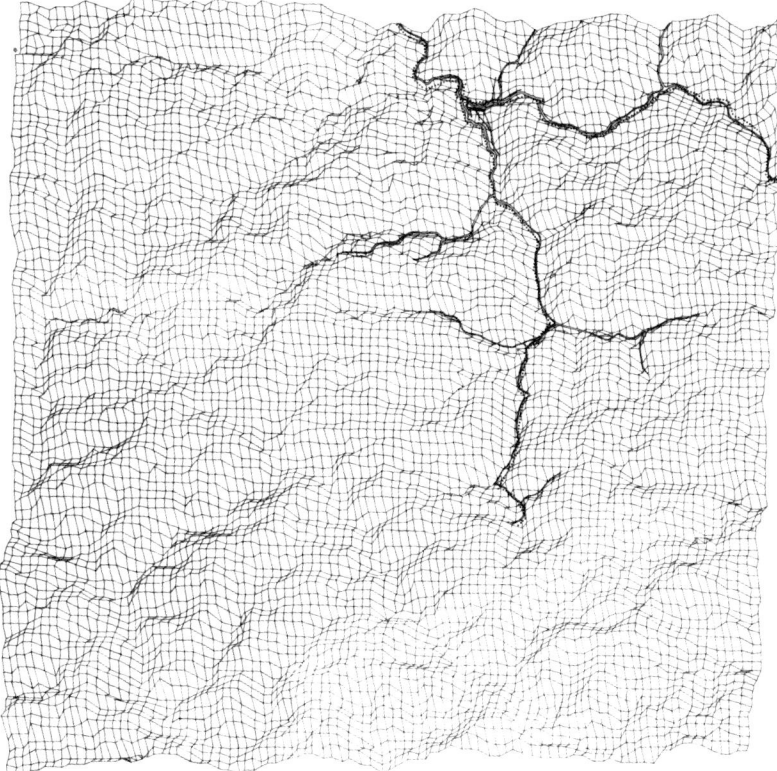

EARLY COMPANY TOWNS OF THE VIRGINIAS - GARY DIGITAL TOPOGRAPHY
United States, West Virginia, Gary (1982)
Digital Drawing

UNITED STATES

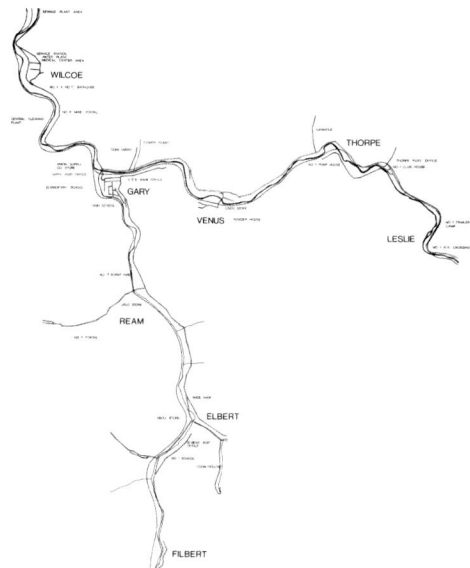

EARLY COMPANY TOWNS OF THE VIRGINIAS - GARY PLAN AND REGIONAL MAP
United States, West Virginia, Gary (1982)
Digital Drawings

THE PARADOX OF PLACE: IN THE LINE OF SIGHT

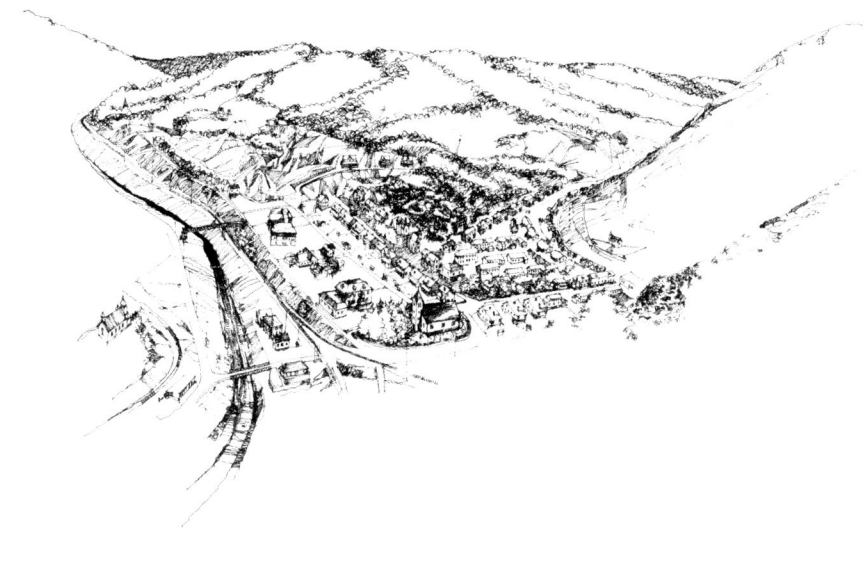

EARLY COMPANY TOWNS OF THE VIRGINIAS - GARY AERIAL SKETCH
United States, West Virginia, Gary (1982)
Pen and Ink Drawing on Fabriano Paper
33.02 cm x 48.26 cm (13 in x 19 in)

UNITED STATES

EARLY COMPANY TOWNS OF THE VIRGINIAS - GARY LINEAR LAYOUT
United States, West Virginia, Gary (1982)
Pen and Ink Drawing on Fabriano Paper
33.02 cm x 48.26 cm (13 in x 19 in)

THE PARADOX OF PLACE: IN THE LINE OF SIGHT

EARLY COMPANY TOWNS OF THE VIRGINIAS - GARY CHURCHES
United States, West Virginia, Gary (1982)
Pen and Ink Drawing on Fabriano Paper
33.02 cm x 48.26 cm (13 in x 19 in)

UNITED STATES

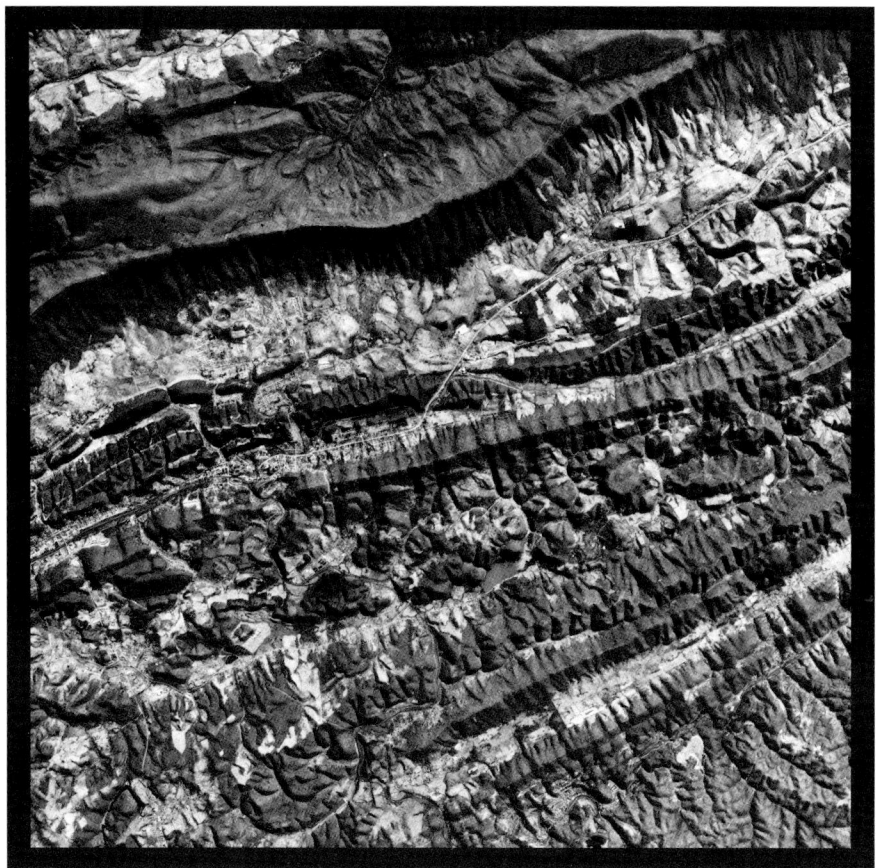

EARLY COMPANY TOWNS OF THE VIRGINIAS - POCAHONTAS AERIAL PHOTOGRAPH
United States, Virginia, Pocahontas (1982)
Aerial Photograph

THE PARADOX OF PLACE: IN THE LINE OF SIGHT

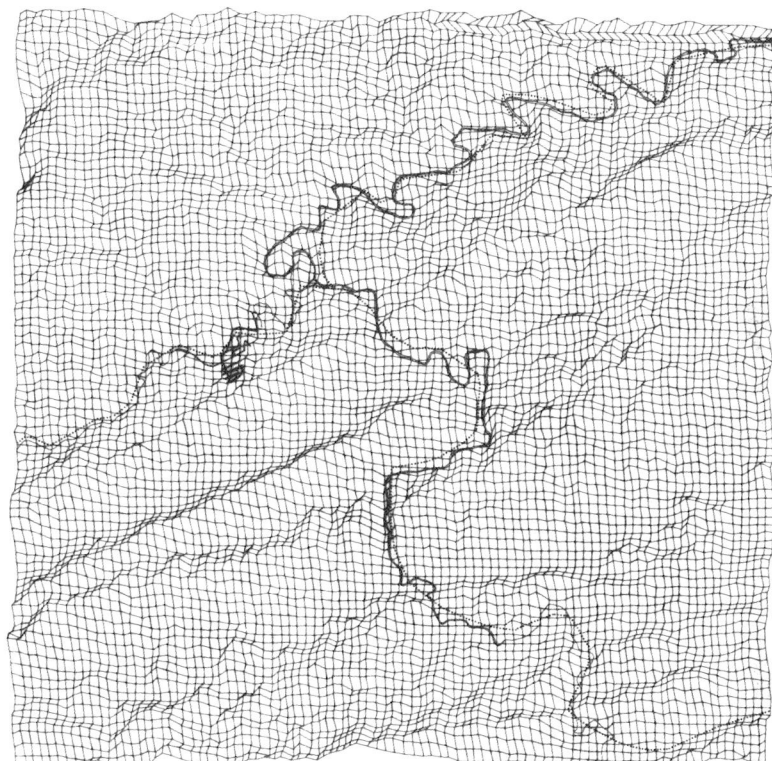

EARLY COMPANY TOWNS OF THE VIRGINIAS - POCAHONTAS DIGITAL TOPOGRAPHY
United States, Virginia, Pocahontas (1982)
Digital Drawing

UNITED STATES

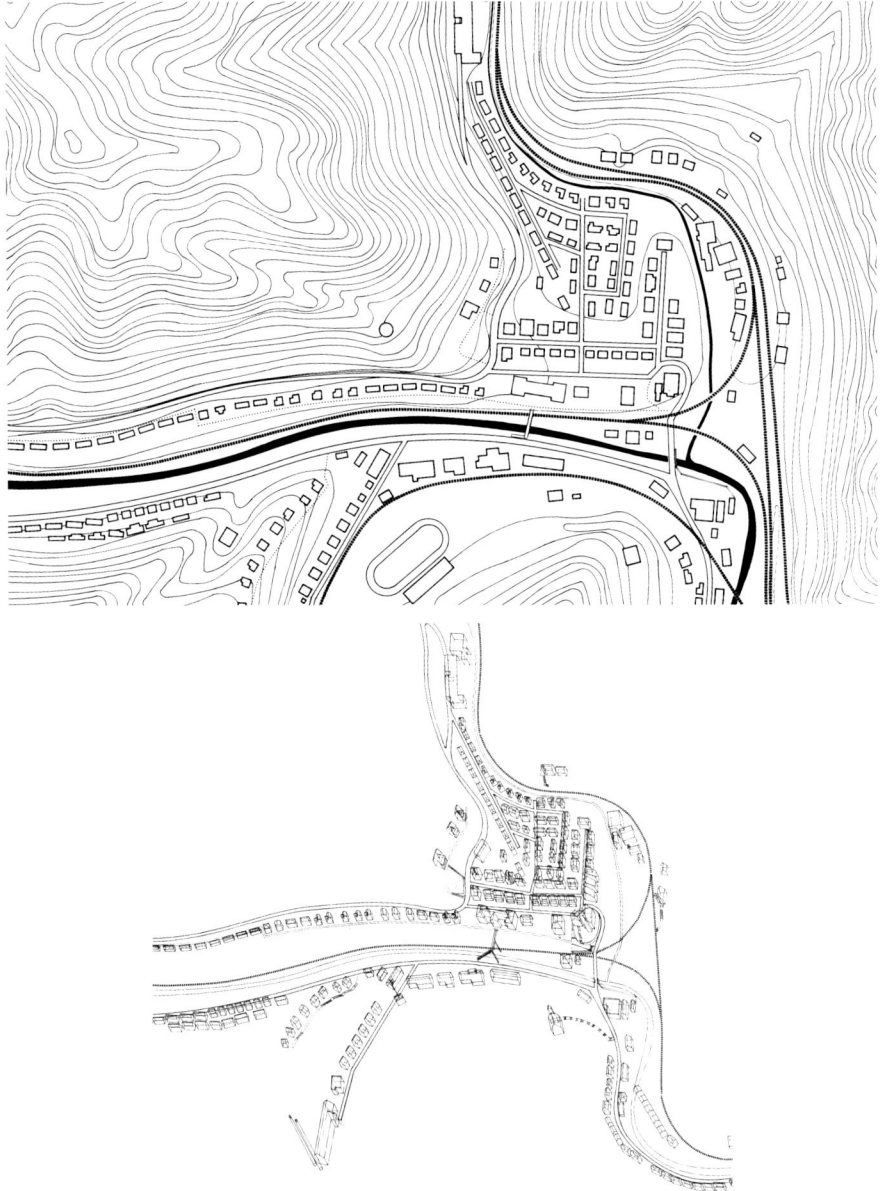

EARLY COMPANY TOWNS OF THE VIRGINIAS - POCAHONTAS PLAN AND AXONOMETRIC
United States, Virginia, Pocahontas (1982)
Digtal Drawing

THE PARADOX OF PLACE: IN THE LINE OF SIGHT

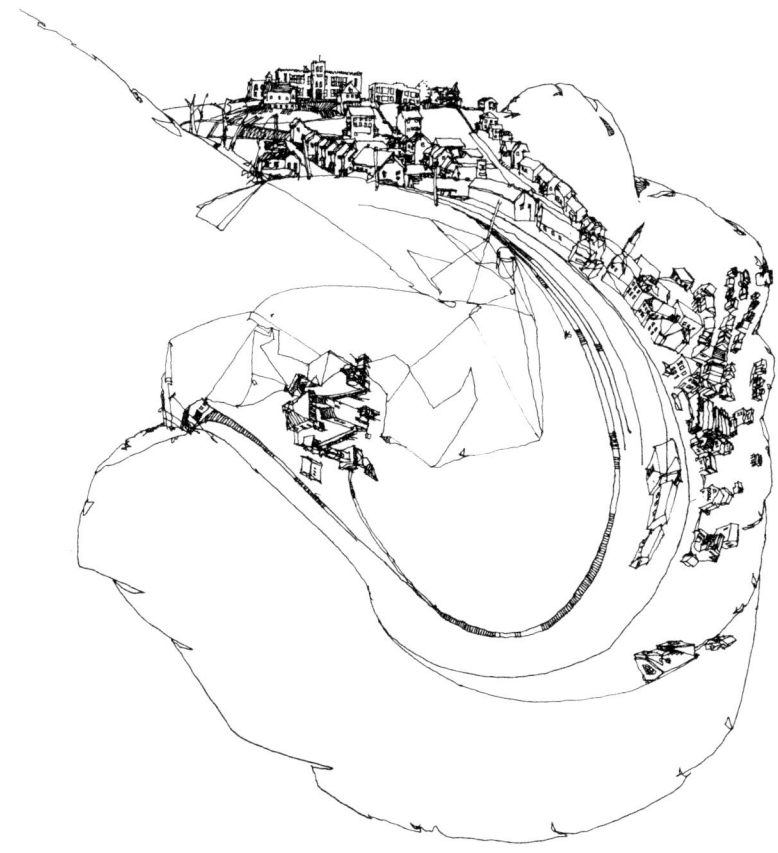

EARLY COMPANY TOWNS OF THE VIRGINIAS - POCAHONTAS AERIAL SKETCH
United States, Virginia, Pocahontas (1982)
Pen and Ink Drawing on Fabriano Paper
33.02 cm x 48.26 cm (13 in x 19 in)

UNITED STATES

EARLY COMPANY TOWNS OF THE VIRGINIAS - POCAHONTAS VIEW FROM SUPERVISOR HOUSE
United States, Virginia, Pocahontas (1982)
Pen and Ink Drawing on Fabriano Paper
33.02 cm x 48.26 cm (13 in x 19 in)

THE PARADOX OF PLACE: IN THE LINE OF SIGHT

EARLY COMPANY TOWNS OF THE VIRGINIAS - POCAHONTAS APPROACH - 01
United States, Virginia, Pocahontas (1982)
Pen and Ink Drawing on Fabriano Paper
33.02 cm x 48.26 cm (13 in x 19 in)

UNITED STATES

EARLY COMPANY TOWNS OF THE VIRGINIAS - POCAHONTAS APPROACH - 02
United States, Virginia, Pocahontas (1982)
Pen and Ink Drawing on Fabriano Paper
33.02 cm x 48.26 cm (13 in x 19 in)

THE PARADOX OF PLACE: IN THE LINE OF SIGHT

EARLY COMPANY TOWNS OF THE VIRGINIAS - POCAHONTAS APPROACH - 03
United States, Virginia, Pocahontas (1982)
Pen and Ink Drawing on Fabriano Paper
33.02 cm x 48.26 cm (13 in x 19 in)

Gregory A. Luhan, Ph.D.

TIMELESSNESS AND CURRENCY
Drawing as an Embodied Signature

Gregory A. Luhan, Ph.D.

> "Every one of us carries a gestural signature – that is either honest or bullshit. I talk to my students about discovering their signature. When they sign their name, is it really about their truth."[1]
> Antoine Predock, in Gregory Luhan Conversations with Antoine Predock

THE INNER IMPULSE | THE TRADITIONAL REGISTERS OF ARCHITECTURE SEPARATE INTO THE ELEMENTS OF DESIGN AND COMMUNICATION and span the spectrum of drawing, modeling, building, speaking, and writing. For the architect, these outlets become a useful medium to translate their inner impulses into ideas and ultimately, into buildings. In a recent conversation with Antoine Predock, he stated "For me, architecture starts with the body and the inner impulse. The inner impulse makes the search apparent; it is cumulative and mystical."[1] For me, the act of drawing is not technical; it is about flow, it is about knowing how the line should be and finding how it needs to be to best convey information about a subject. There's nothing mysterious about it, but it is personal. For Dayton Eugene Egger, the drawing is a public work that is personal, but not private. The way that this process often reveals itself is not necessarily as rigorous as how one would train for marathons or other activities. But it also isn't something that lands on you from out of nowhere; it is something that a great teacher brings out of you naturally; a combination of intuition and instruction. A great teacher influences a student by lighting a fire and by situating them in inspiring contexts to learn, however, it is really about you, the student, who discovers that internal voice. For me, Dayton Eugene Egger was that first great teacher. Professor Egger was both the first person and the last person that I met as a student at Virginia Tech. Since that first day, Gene served as my mentor and career guide. As a sounding board, he always challenged me to see deeper into my work in order to tap the creative process, to pursue innovation, and to find my inner spirit.

BRACKETING THE SKETCHBOOK | Our goal as architects is to represent the world as tangible spaces that are inhabitable. Egger always challenged us to draw simultaneously in both plan and section, as the plan is where we move and the section is where we live. For Egger, the section was a structural way of searching for understanding one's context. This concept of fulfillment conveys the sensibility of immersing oneself in a culture. It enables us to understand the world in contours. When we draw in section, we find the visceral elements and layers of form. The section adeptly serves as an immersive device that allows us to rethink the environment. When we capture space, we are drawing not only the ground but the edges and surfaces that comprise the background, foreground, and degrees of middleground as well as how these elements set against the sky. When we depict the space in which we situate, we convey distance; presenting things that are far away with less detail, while presenting things that are closer with more information. Egger challenged us to realize that walls have two sides and a center. Walls can take on the character of a place; they are not abstract representations. The notion of the wall as having a presence that speaks to and absorbs both sides of a wall means that it is a bridge between two distinct phenomena. Egger refers to this concept as "platial," a term that builds upon Bruno Zevi's theory of architecture and space as a discursive component that describes a process of becoming linked to sensory experience.

> "When I look at one of my drawings it suggests the smell of the sea or whatever I was adjacent to; it evokes the time of day and reveals the way that light strikes a surface."
> Antoine Predock, in Gregory Luhan *Conversations with Antoine Predock*

Alvin Noe describes the sensory experience as transparently reflective of one's encounter with the world. For Egger, the drawing is a willful and calculated act of architecture; an enactive representation imbued with compositional strategies such as scale and proportion. Often his diaphanous sketches are near-Cubist expressions that depict architectural values from a plurality of perspectives. The resulting pictorial representations, such as those featured in this book, depict spaces, places, and events simultaneously and from multiple vantage points so that one's vision and thought process "comingle on the page."[2] Egger's images actively link the site's cultural legacy as an articulation of the social and cultural context that shapes thought processes through drawing. Bruno Zevi describes these conveyances as "spatial interpretations"[3] that communicate the essence of architecture. Egger would often use the sketch to teach students how to acquire knowledge through experience. For Egger, the sketches are concurrent visual expressions and connective tissues that bridge the site to the classroom through sectional occupation. The sketch, therefore, is an interactive teaching tool that has the potential for enhanced discovery.

Gregory A. Luhan, Ph.D.

MAKING POSITIVE LINES | Today, we draw with many mediums and do so in a very controlled way. For architects to draw well, we must be willing to fully embrace failure by not necessarily anticipating outcomes, but instead, by building the drawing. To align with Antoine's words, one must have an inner impulse guiding the mark. It is essential for us to understand the context by capturing the motion of the place. The quality of the line is the architect's contact with the character of a place. Often this means working with lines in response to place. Egger regularly described the necessity of making the line positive, active, and alive to demonstrate movement in layers. In this way, the drawing is a place unto itself, evidence of the incessant struggle to get lineweight into the drawing in the hopes of revealing the "textures of the built environment."[4] Architects convey vertical tension, pictorial quality, and the contrast between material, slope, landscape, and the concrete world through sketching. As Egger would characterize it, when we draw, we capture not only the edges and mass but also the spaces between objects. To him, the drawing was a thinking medium, a combination of precision and incompleteness that expresses detail, contour, and profile. The drawing develops over time. The concept of time in a drawing captures the sense of wonder. We must look at the context slowly to create the densities and tones that express the landscape that we are trying to replicate. The drawing and the quality of the line reveal the

PLACES OF PLACE: SKETCHING THE ENCOUNTER EXHIBITION
Commonwealth Gallery - Downtown Arts Center, Lexington, KY (11 September 2016)
Photograph, Gregory Luhan

order and the flow of the space. Therefore, it isn't difficult for us to articulate intersections between the wall, the ground between the wall, and the pavement.

"Drawings are journals." Antoine Predock, in Gregory Luhan Conversations with Antoine Predock

THE PAGE IS THE REALITY OF THE ARCHITECT'S INTERPRETATION. Gene Egger embraces the sketch as a visual journal that records and strengthens one's confrontation with the essential invisible phenomenon of the site. The drawing, in a sense, is not only about documenting the historical precedent but also about capturing the quality and the character of a place. To do so, the architect or student must be in the moment of the site. For Gene and those who have traveled or studied with him, it is about understanding, honoring, and delivering on one's responsibility to a place. This process is challenging (and undoubtedly rare), but it also elevates the act of drawing to an experiential event. It is less about clinically documenting a building than about taking it in and soaking it up, and then conveying it through gestural lines. To understand the process of drawing is to understand how the representation emerges from the strata of place and how it works its way up through the thin film of cultural intervention. The sketch, therefore, simultaneously expresses both the cultural history and the possible future of a place. The drawing is a way of conveying one's

PLACES OF PLACE: SKETCHING THE ENCOUNTER EXHIBITION
Commonwealth Gallery - Downtown Arts Center, Lexington, KY (11 September 2016)
Photograph, Gregory Luhan

Gregory A. Luhan, Ph.D.

world as a sequence of living experiences that connects through space. Sketches translate information through gestural movements that loosely suggested what one would see but differed entirely from what one would express in a photograph.

Drawing is not a subject; but rather, it is an organic event that liberates the line, regardless of its format. Drawing is an episodic design; an accumulating storyboard that comes to life through the process of drawing. In architecture, one must identify a subject. Gene always advised us to start first with finding an object of interest and framing it such that it tantalizes visual and spatial interest. Upon finding the subject, the drawing begins with the first line of the page. Usually, this line, drawn top to bottom or right to left, describes the type of space vertical or horizontal. This line is a reference to which all other lines respond, noting that the first mark on the page predicts the next line. The following line builds upon and responds to the previous line allowing the architect to extract characteristics and to understand the page as a set of layers. As the drawing develops, the architect continues to add spatial complexity while increasing environmental combinations that fill the page. Drawings, while they work on the page, are usually finished off of the page. In this way, the sketch or drawing is more construction than representation, and the lines are the notations of interpretation and experience.

UKY DESIGN STUDENTS | CONVERSATIONS WITH DAYTON EUGENE EGGER
Midway, KY (14 September 2016)
Photograph, Allison May

In the 50 years since Olivio Ferrari and Charles Burchard recruited Gene to Virginia Tech, he led thousands of students on the college's international study abroad program. He documented the experiences of being away from campus through drawing and leveraged educational tools in a way that wouldn't have been possible by staying only in Blacksburg. Of course, he also used those same techniques to examine and understand the mining towns of Virginia and West Virginia and translated those opportunities into a series of analytical experiments using both drawing and photography. In 2016, Gene extended this research into Kentucky. The Kentucky landscape is a fantastic landscape that is in a perpetual search for a horizon line. This context is meant to be both inhabitable and open to the sky. As architects, we love it; live it, and breathe it. When Gene came to Lexington for *The Places of Place: Sketching the Encounter Exhibition*, he met with and talked to more than one hundred University of Kentucky (UKY) College of Design students and then delivered a well-attended public lecture. The experience that I crafted for him during his time in the Commonwealth enabled him to visit the small towns of rural Kentucky with forty students, many of whom had never been to these architecturally rich contexts. The trips required students to rethink how they traditionally document a site. Students were very quick to want to whip out their cameras or smartphones and start taking pictures only to be reminded that on this day, the weapon of choice was the pen and the technique; controlling one's breathing, almost meditating, and drawing out the moment. One site was the Wild Turkey Distillery, in Lawrenceburg – an Acropolis-like setting with its monumental bourbon warehouses high atop the Palisades with the sinuous Kentucky River below. Another was Midway, a small train town with an active Main Street and a dynamic elevational change pierced by rail lines. Gene's conversations with the students centered on confronting the site and translating vital visual phenomena of the places – not necessarily as a fixed object but alternatively as a visual immersion that inhabits the site. The drawings conveyed information not only through the lines on the page, but also communicated the overall experience of its creation. The framework outlined by Gene during his Kentucky trip reinforced what served as a guide for my professional and academic career for over thirty years and still inspires me today, indeed proving that architecture is extraordinary and timeless.

NOTES

[1] Luhan, G.A. (2017, January 12). Personal Interview with Antoine Predock [Antoine Predock, Architect].
[2] Noë, A. (2004). *Action in perception* (Representation and mind). Cambridge, MA: MIT Press.
[3] Zevi, B. (1957). *Architecture as space; how to look at architecture.* New York: Horizon Press.
[4] (1999). Herb Greene: A Discussion with Richard Levine in *2 days – 40 years: "flashback/flashforward: Architecture and urbanism 1960-2000": A symposium to commemorate forty years of architecture at the University of Kentucky.* Lexington, KY: Office of the Dean, College of Architecture, University of Kentucky.

Gregory A. Luhan, Ph.D.

DAYTON EUGENE EGGER
*Midway, KY (14 September 2016)
Photograph, Allison May*

TIMELESSNESS AND CURRENCY | Drawing as an Embodied Signature

DAYTON EUGENE EGGER | POST-SKETCH REVIEW WITH UKY DESIGN STUDENTS
Midway, KY (14 September 2016)
Photograph, Allison May

208

EUROPE PROGRAMS
1969-2018

STUDY ABROAD - EUROPE PROGRAMS - 1969-2018

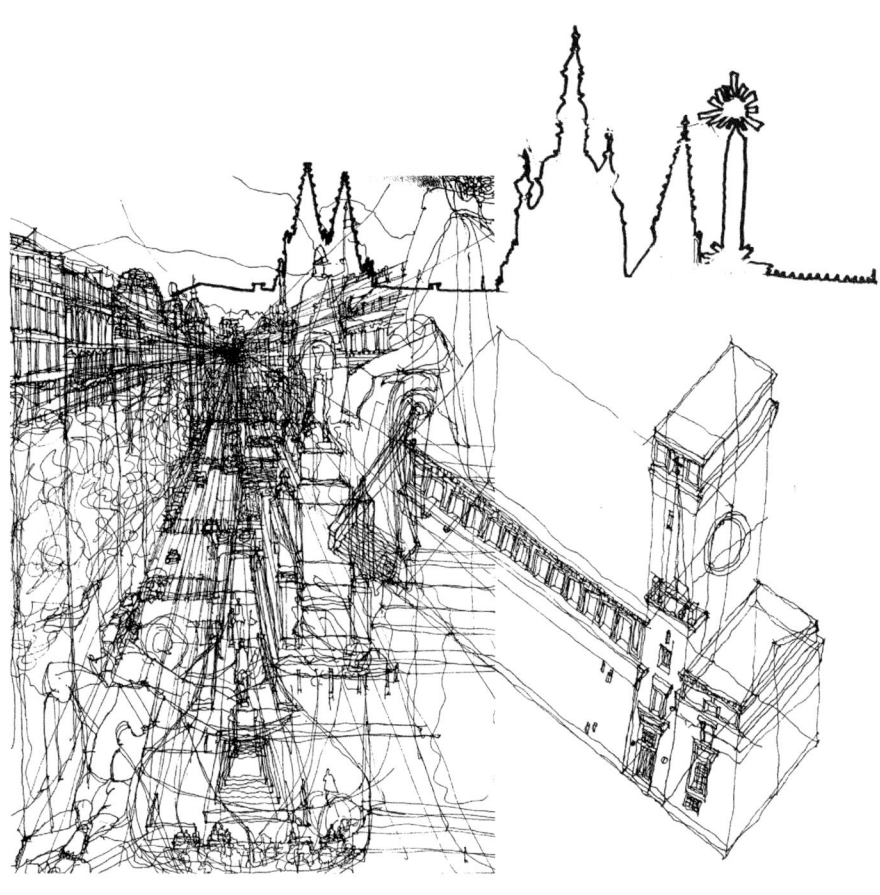

EUROPE PROGRAMS - 1969-2018 | PRAGUE
Europe, Czech Republic, Prague - Natalie Wigginton (Undated)
Pen and Ink Drawing on Fabriano Paper
33.02 cm x 48.26 cm (13 in x 19 in)

THE PARADOX OF PLACE: IN THE LINE OF SIGHT

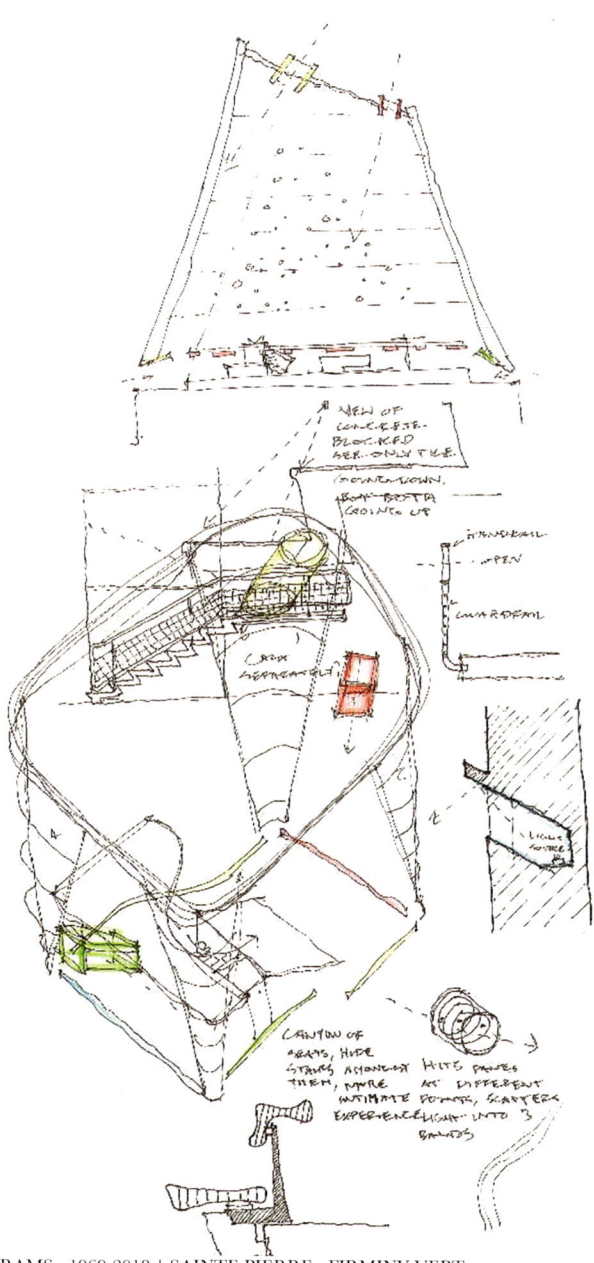

EUROPE PROGRAMS - 1969-2018 | SAINTE PIERRE - FIRMINY VERT
Europe, France, Firminy - Jason Andrews (Fall 2017)
Pen and Ink Drawing with Color Pencil on Arches Paper
22.86 cm x 30.48 cm (9 in x 12 in)

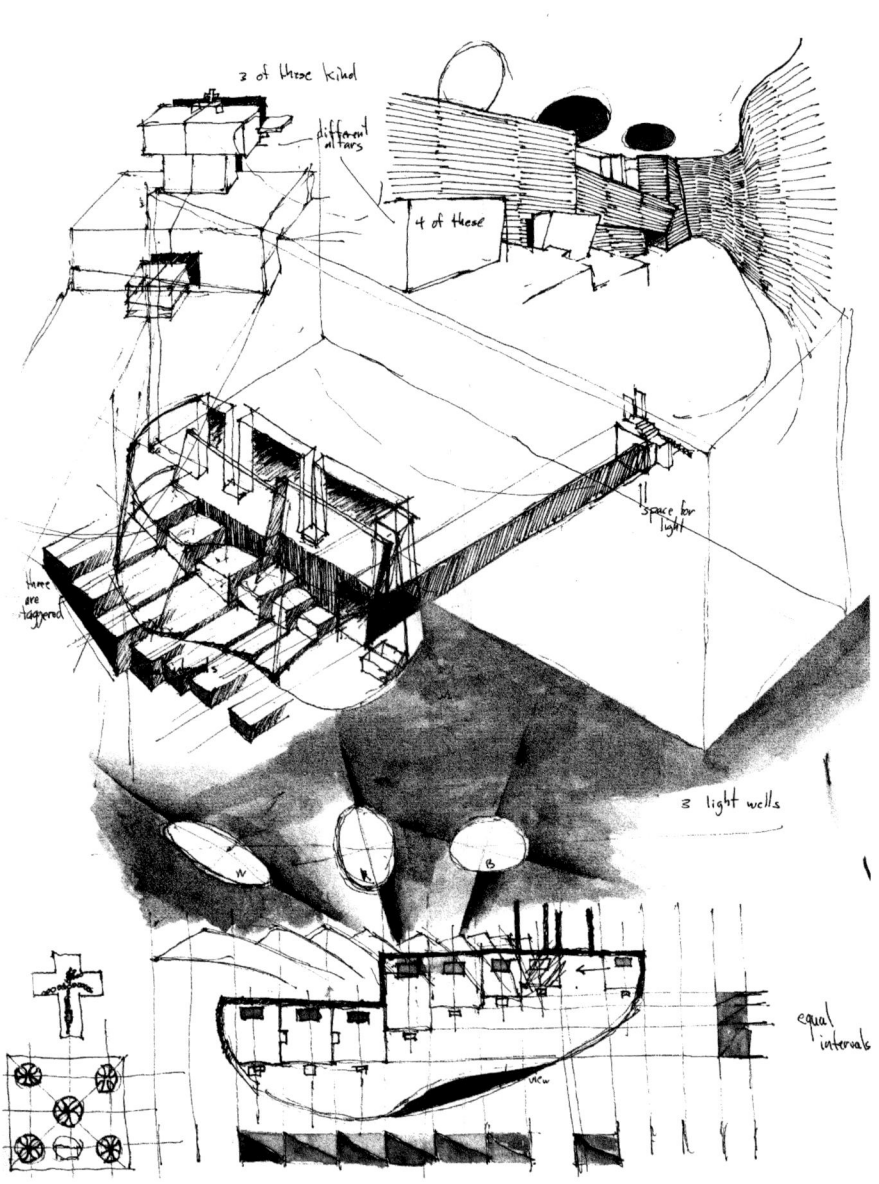

EUROPE PROGRAMS - 1969-2018 | SAINTE MARIE DE LA TOURETTE
Europe, France, L'Arbresle - Nasser Abulhasan (1998)
Mixed Media, Pen and Ink with Pencil Drawing on Fabriano Paper
33.02 cm x 48.26 cm (13 in x 19 in)

THE PARADOX OF PLACE: IN THE LINE OF SIGHT

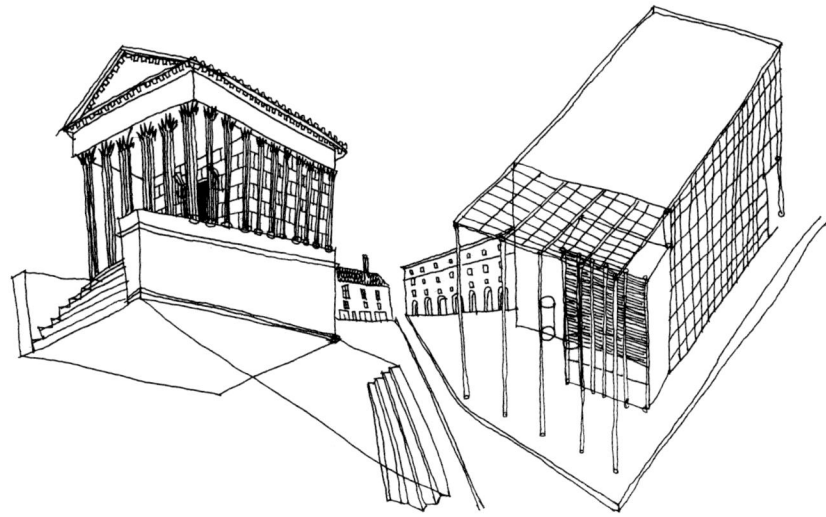

EUROPE PROGRAMS - 1969-2018 | MAISON CARREE D'ART
Europe, France, Nimes - Daniel Cryer (Fall 2015)
Pen and Ink Drawing on Arches Paper
30.48 cm x 22.86 cm (12 in x 9 in)

STUDY ABROAD - EUROPE PROGRAMS - 1969-2018

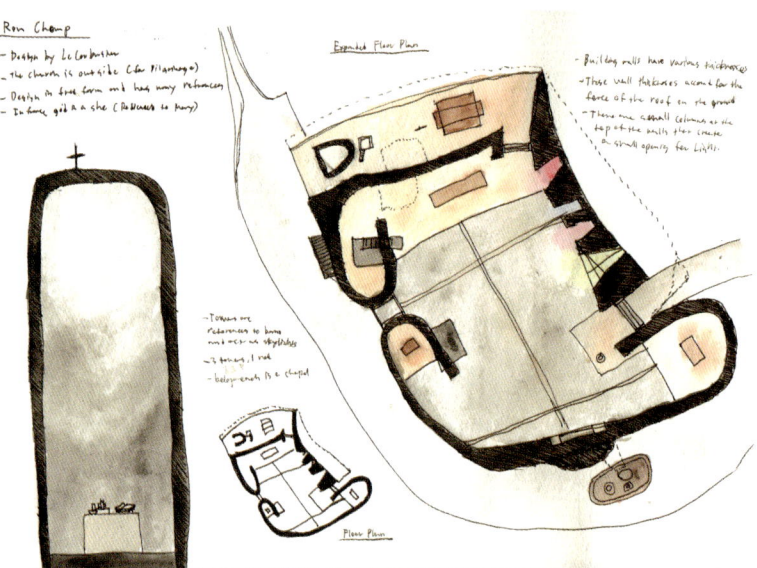

EUROPE PROGRAMS - 1969-2018 | NOTRE DAME DU HAUT
Europe, France, Ronchamp - Michael Mckonen (Fall 2014)
Pen and Ink Drawing with Color Pencil and Watercolor Wash on Arches Paper
22.86 cm x 30.48 cm (9 in x 12 in)

THE PARADOX OF PLACE: IN THE LINE OF SIGHT

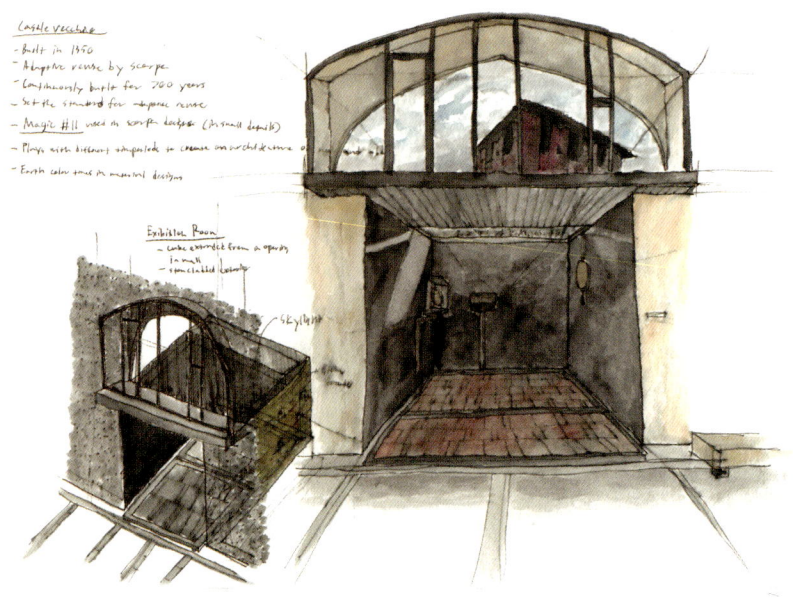

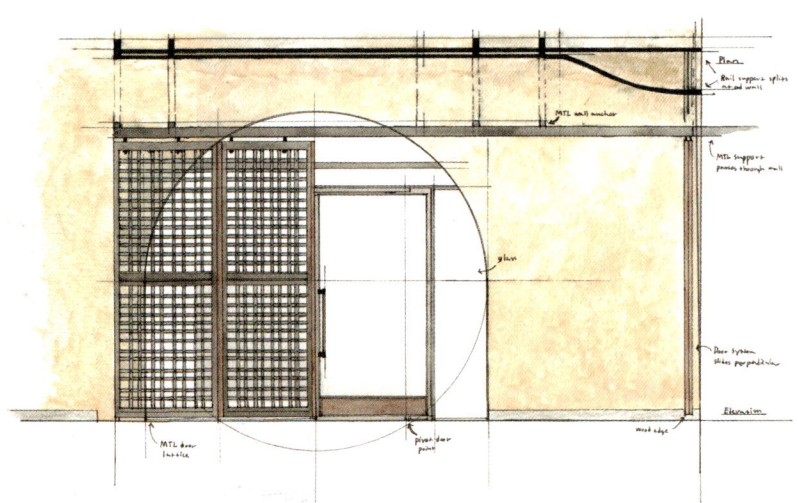

EUROPE PROGRAMS - 1969-2018 | CASTELVECCHIO MUSEUM
Europe, Italy, Verona - Michael Mckonen (Fall 2014)
Pen and Ink Drawing with Color Pencil and Watercolor Wash on Arches Paper
33.02 cm x 48.26 cm (13 in x 19 in)

215

STUDY ABROAD - EUROPE PROGRAMS - 1969-2018

EUROPE PROGRAMS - 1969-2018 | CHIESA DI SANT'IVO ALLA SAPIENZA
Europe, Italy, Rome - Daniel Cryer (Fall 2015)
Pen and Ink Drawing on Arches Paper
22.86 cm x 30.48 cm (9 in x 12 in)

THE PARADOX OF PLACE: IN THE LINE OF SIGHT

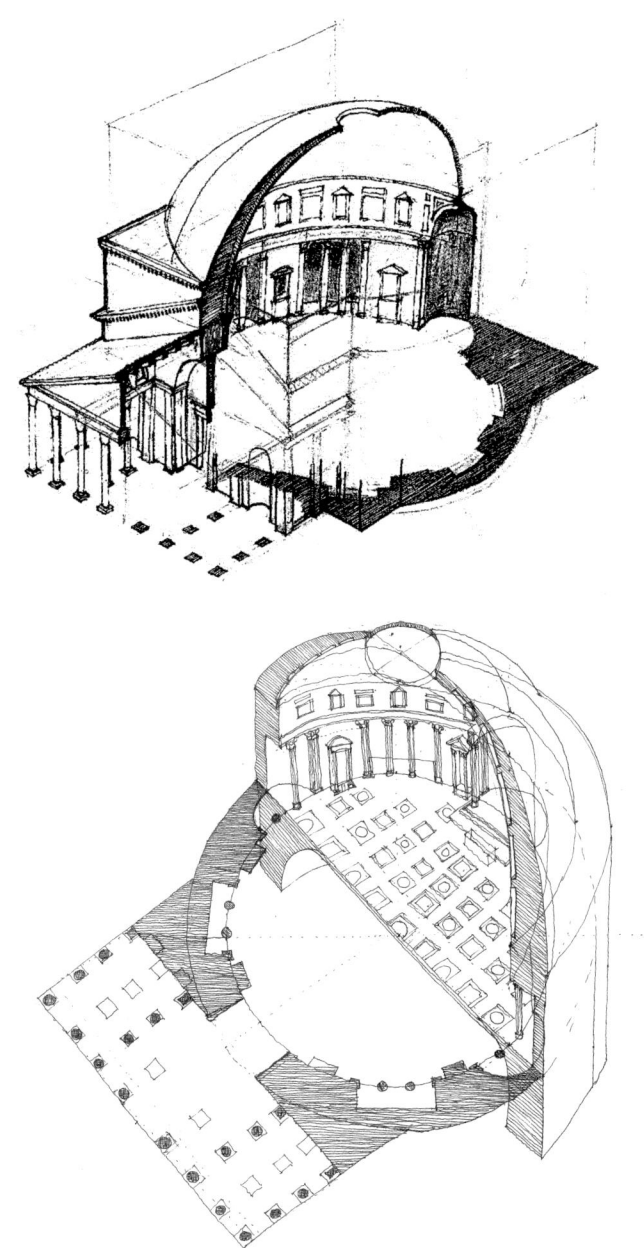

EUROPE PROGRAMS - 1969-2018 | PANTHEON
Europe, Italy, Rome - Kirsten Sparenborg (Fall 2000) (top); Jason Andrews (Fall 2017) (bottom)
Pencil Drawing on Fabriano Paper; Pencil Drawing on Arches Paper
33.02 cm x 48.26 cm (13 in x 19 in)

STUDY ABROAD - EUROPE PROGRAMS - 1969-2018

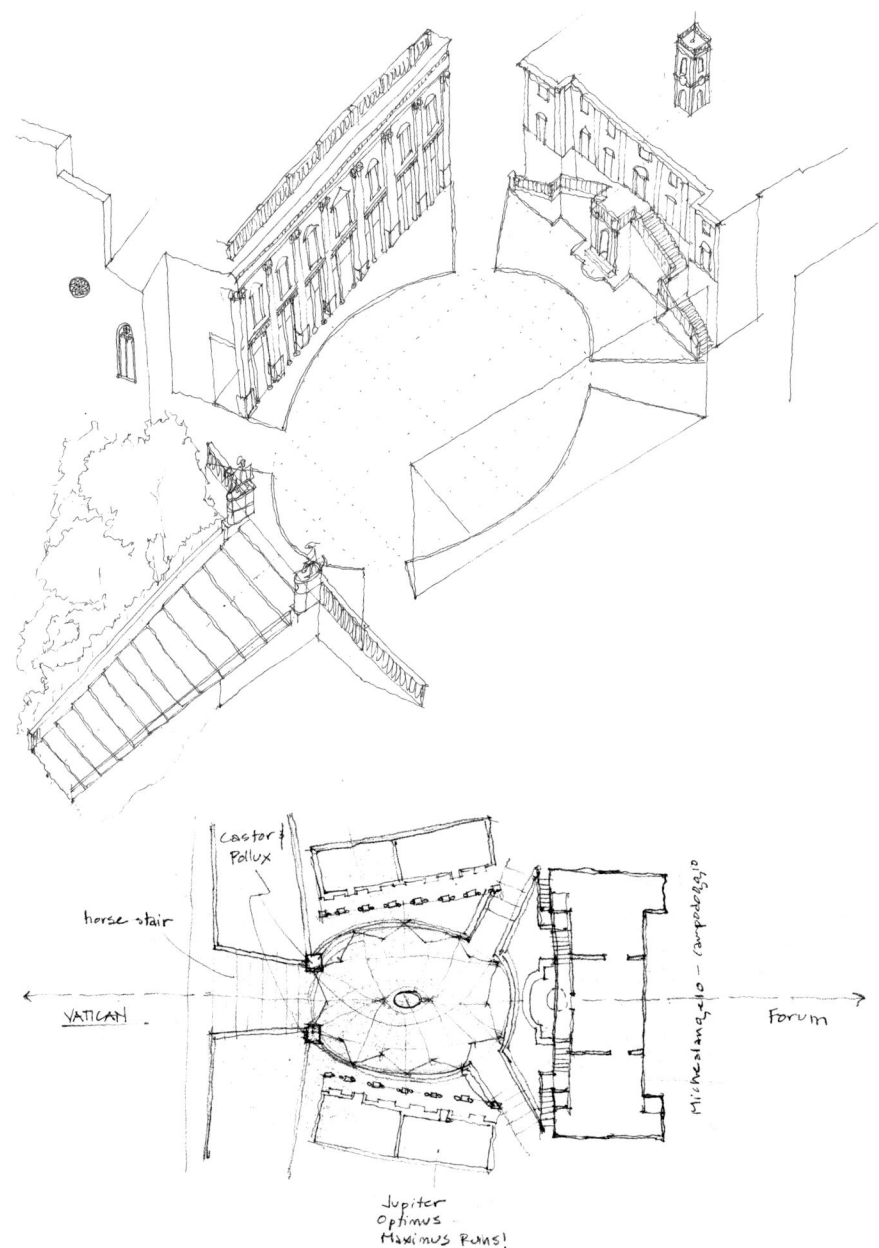

EUROPE PROGRAMS - 1969-2018 | PIAZZA DEL CAMPIDOGLIO - CAPITOLINE HILL
Europe, Italy, Rome - Jason Andrews (top); Trey King (bottom) (Fall 2017)
Pencil Drawing on Arches Paper Sketchbook; Pencil Drawing on Arches Paper Sketchbook
22.86 cm x 30.48 cm (9 in x 12 in); 22.86 cm x 30.48 cm (9 in x 12 in)

THE PARADOX OF PLACE: IN THE LINE OF SIGHT

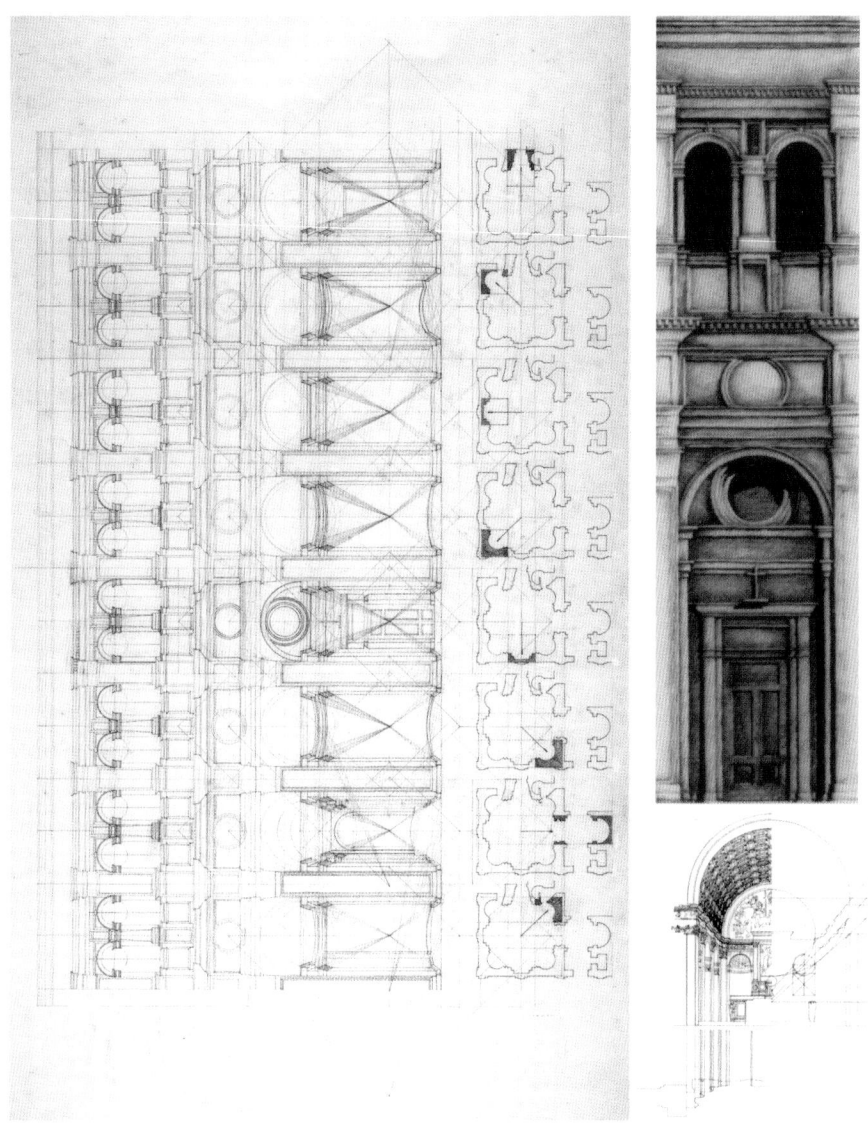

EUROPE PROGRAMS - 1969-2018 | CHIESA DI SANTA MARIA PRESSO SAN SATIRO
Europe, Italy, Milan - Gregory Luhan (Fall 1997)
Pencil Drawing on Vellum; Pencil Drawing on Fabriano Paper; Pen and Ink Drawing on Fabriano Paper
91.44 cm x 182.88 cm (36 in x 72 in); 33.02 cm x 48.26 cm (13 in x 19 in); 33.02 cm x 48.26 cm (13 in x 19 in)

STUDY ABROAD - EUROPE PROGRAMS - 1969-2018

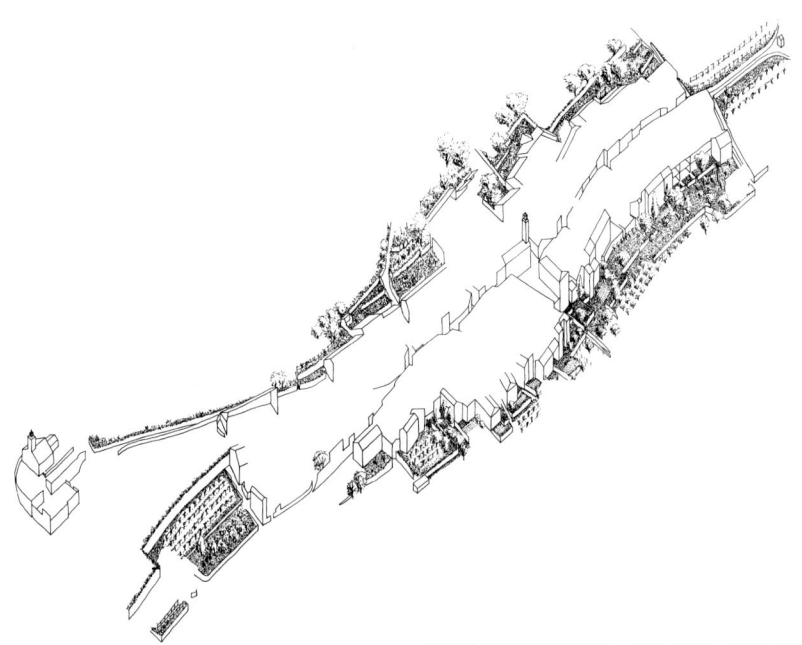

EUROPE PROGRAMS - 1969-2018 | MERIDE - 01
Europe, Italy, Meride - Darren DeGood (Undated) (top); Darren DeGood (11 November 1991) (bottom)
Pen and Ink Drawing on Fabriano Paper; Pen and Ink Drawing on Fabriano Paper
33.02 cm x 48.26 cm (13 in x 19 in); 33.02 cm x 48.26 cm (13 in x 19 in)

THE PARADOX OF PLACE: IN THE LINE OF SIGHT

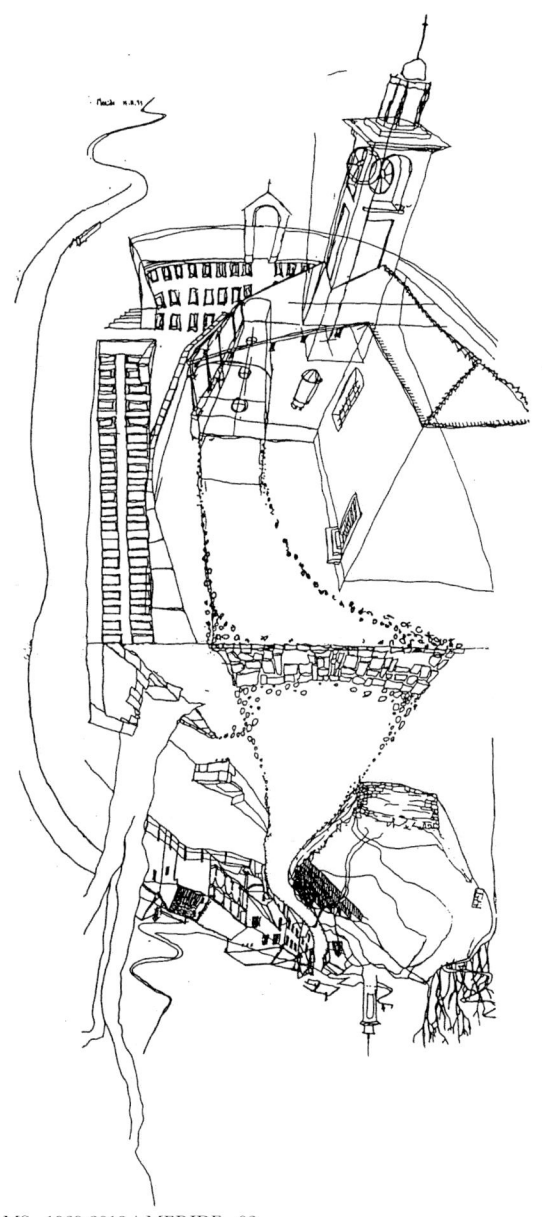

EUROPE PROGRAMS - 1969-2018 | MERIDE - 02
Europe, Italy, Meride - Thom White (11 November 1991)
Pen and Ink Drawing on Fabriano Paper
33.02 cm x 48.26 cm (13 in x 19 in)

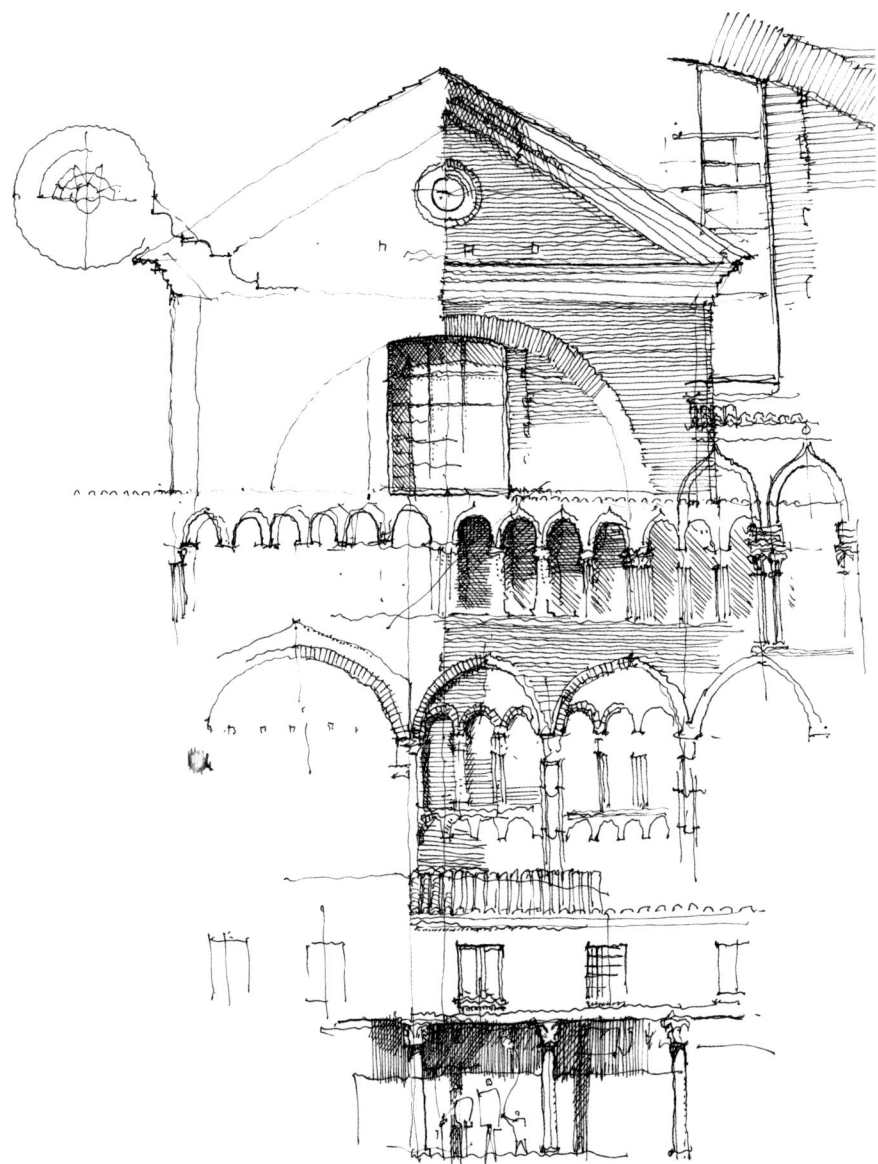

EUROPE PROGRAMS - 1969-2018 | BASILICA CATTEDRALE DI SAN GIORGIO, DUOMO DI FERRARA
Europe, Italy, Ferrara - Mark Blizard (04 April 2018)
Pen and Ink Drawing in Moleskine Sketchbook
20.995 cm x 28.575 cm (8.25 in x 11.25 in)

THE PARADOX OF PLACE: IN THE LINE OF SIGHT

EUROPE PROGRAMS - 1969-2018 | BASILICA OF SAN VITALE
Europe, Italy, Ravenna- Mark Blizard (29 March 2018)
Pen and Ink Drawing in Moleskine Sketchbook
20.995 cm x 28.575 cm (8.25 in x 11.25 in)

STUDY ABROAD - EUROPE PROGRAMS - 1969-2018

EUROPE PROGRAMS - 1969-2018 | ASSISI - 01
Europe, Italy, Assisi - Steven House (13 July 1982)
Pen and Ink Drawing with Watercolor Wash on Fabriano Paper
33.02 cm x 48.26 cm (13 in x 19 in)

THE PARADOX OF PLACE: IN THE LINE OF SIGHT

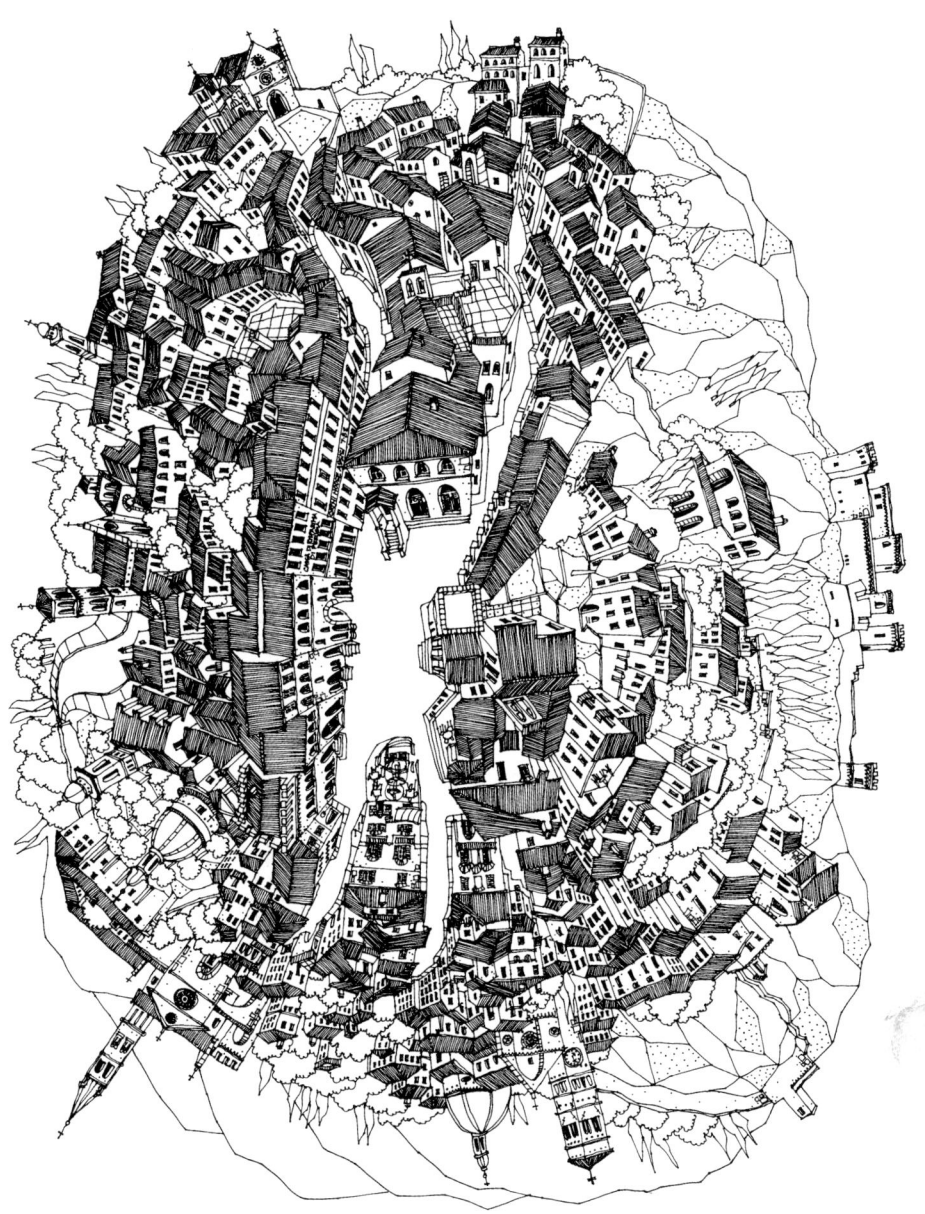

EUROPE PROGRAMS - 1969-2018 | ASSISI - 02
Europe, Italy, Assisi - Cathi House (14 July 1982)
Pen and Ink Drawing on Fabriano Paper
33.02 cm x 48.26 cm (13 in x 19 in)

STUDY ABROAD - EUROPE PROGRAMS - 1969-2018

EUROPE PROGRAMS - 1969-2018
Europe, Italy, Capri - Emily Guerin (Undated)
Pen and Ink Drawing on Fabriano Paper
33.02 cm x 48.26 cm (13 in x 19 in)

THE PARADOX OF PLACE: IN THE LINE OF SIGHT

EUROPE PROGRAMS - 1969-2018 | SANTA CROCE CHAPEL
Europe, Switzerland, Riva San Vitale - Patricia Conrad (Undated)
Pen and Ink Drawing on Fabriano Paper
33.02 cm x 48.26 cm (13 in x 19 in)

STUDY ABROAD - EUROPE PROGRAMS - 1969-2018

EUROPE PROGRAMS - 1969-2018 | RIVA SAN VITALE
Europe, Switzerland, Riva San Vitale - Darren DeGood (Undated) (top), (middle); (bottom)
Pen and Ink Drawing on Fabriano Paper
33.02 cm x 48.26 cm (13 in x 19 in)

THE PARADOX OF PLACE: IN THE LINE OF SIGHT

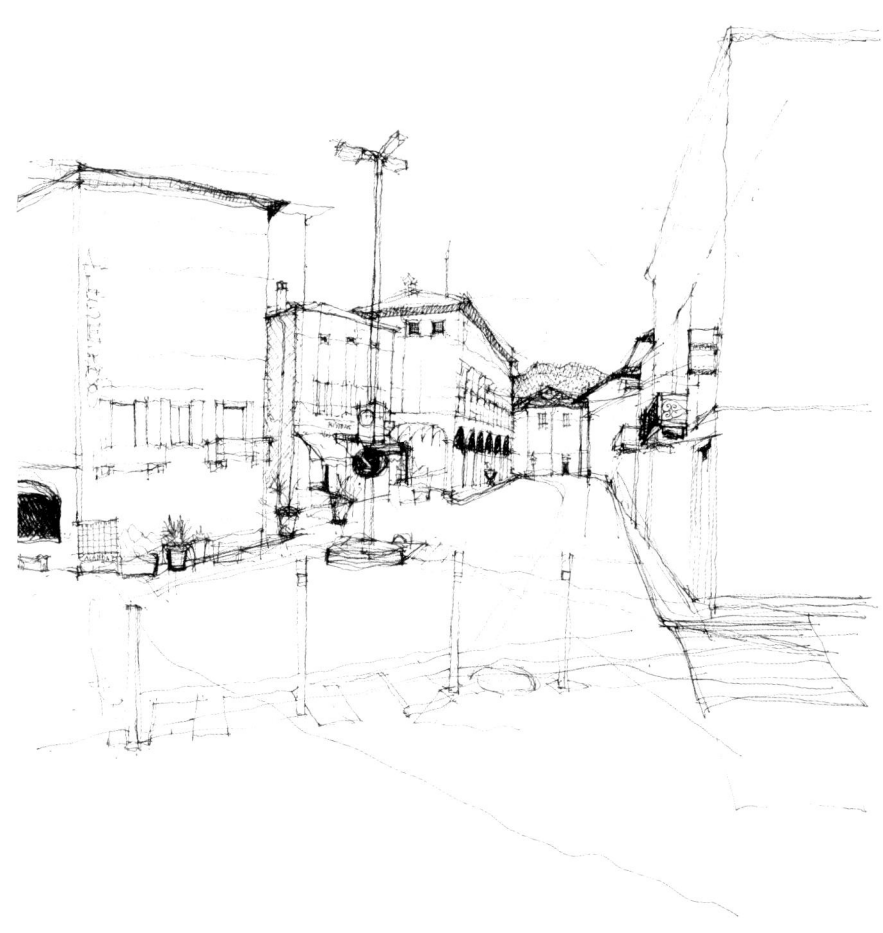

EUROPE PROGRAMS - 1969-2018 | RIVA SAN VITALE - PIAZZA GRANDE
Switzerland, Riva San Vitale (Ticino); Misti Moser (01 May 1995)
Pen and Ink Drawing on Fabriano Paper
33.02 cm x 48.26 cm (13 in x 19 in)

STUDY ABROAD - EUROPE PROGRAMS - 1969-2018

EUROPE PROGRAMS - 1969-2018 | ARCHITECTURE TO FORM - POTTERY STUDY - 01
North America, Texas, San Antonio - Mark Blizard (1998)
Pen and Ink Drawing with Colored Pencil in Canson Sketchbook, 65# paper
13.97 cm x 21.59 cm (5.5 in x 8.5 in)

THE PARADOX OF PLACE: IN THE LINE OF SIGHT

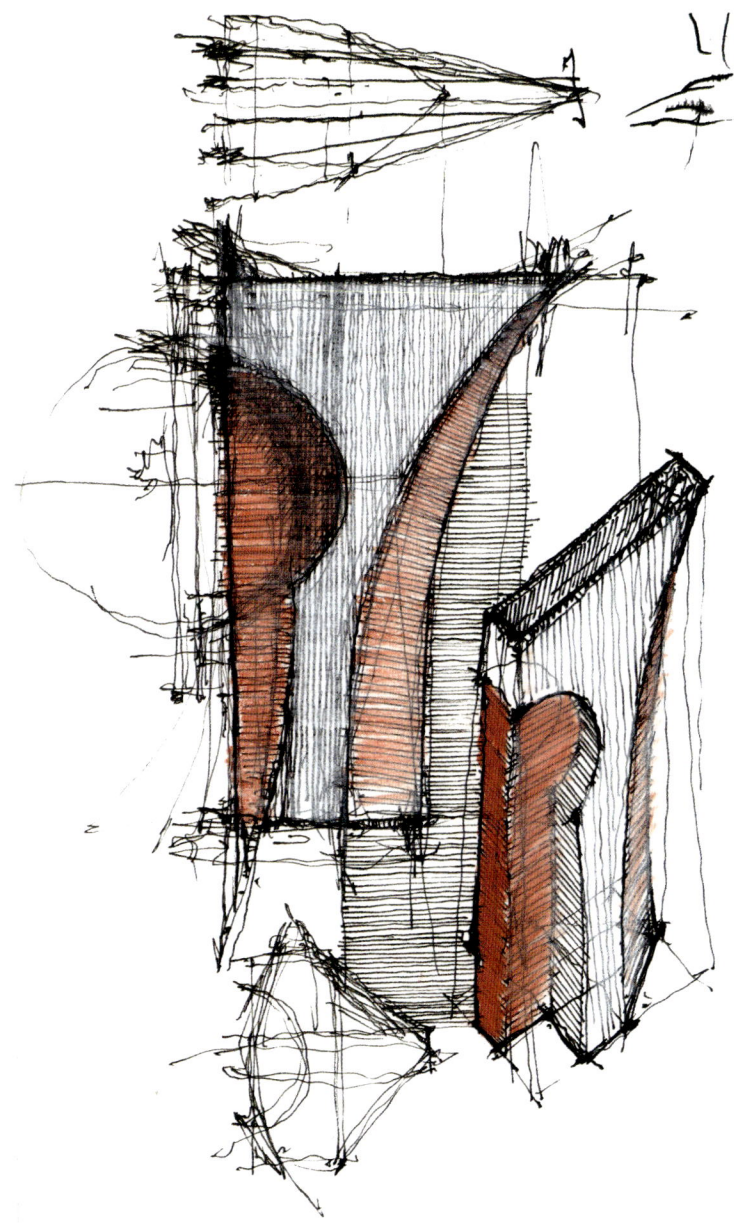

EUROPE PROGRAMS - 1969-2018 | ARCHITECTURE TO FORM - POTTERY STUDY - 02
North America, Texas, San Antonio - Mark Blizard (1998)
Pen and Ink Drawing with Colored Pencil in Canson Sketchbook, 65# paper
13.97 cm x 21.59 cm (5.5 in x 8.5 in)

Frank H. Weiner

AFTERWORD | THE PEDAGOGY OF THE SKETCH

Frank H. Weiner

> *"…every 'being' is a potential for a 'becoming.'"*
> Alfred North Whitehead in *Process and Reality*

TO WRITE ABOUT SKETCHING, IN THIS CASE, THE TRAVEL SKETCHES OF PROFESSOR EUGENE EGGER is an act of high irony. It would amount to making a description of a description – thrice removed from the original building or place sketched. Here one is close to the Platonic dilemma of the doctrine of Ideas or Forms where the only way forward is through mimesis or imitation. In this sense, the sketches are not copies of any kind. They are the wavering lineaments of opinions about what pedagogy looks like and how it appears in the space of the world. The word "sketch" is chosen cautiously as it betrays in its apparent spontaneous informality a well-practiced discipline and study.

The only truly appropriate and worthy architectonic response to a sketch is another sketch. This approach is, in fact, the real contribution of Professor Egger. He has given intelligent form to his entire didactic life in an age where research prowess and over publication overwhelms the gentle efficacy of the art of teaching a visual tradition. However, the limits of the world of written language may shed some light on the rather remarkable selection of pedagogical sketches of Professor Egger. It is important to note most of these sketches were made while he was leading study abroad programs beginning in 1970 and continuing to 2011 in what today is named the School of Architecture + Design at Virginia Tech.

The phrase "pedagogical sketches" typifies a teaching philosophy grounded in the hand-drawn line as a compositional strategy that is less about documenting history and more about an exquisite confrontation with the environs of place. The finely drawn sketches are even more significant when viewed as exemplars of a position about teaching architecture through the encounter of a formal travel program as an integral part of a professional curriculum in architecture.

The sketches are not historical studies or archaeological investigations. Excised from time, they describe the structure of architectural environments, human settlements and the relational processes implicit in such visual settings. The sketches in effect actively design places studied rather than record them. Poised between perspectival and cubist sensibilities they depict the act of design as an act of co-present possibility and a denegation of the weight of actualities. The latent potential of the sketches give perspective to a type of cubist pedagogical space.

Any school of architecture is only as good as the structure of its biases and beliefs provided by the faculty underlying the curriculum. Professor Egger draws from these 'hermeneutic' biases alongside his students so they can discover theirs. At Virginia Tech the primary tendency has been towards travel and away from history. One studies the buildings and places they visit so that when they design they virtually travel to a place that they have never been with increased confidence. Along with these biases is a focus on the education of an architect above even architecture itself. Virginia Tech prides itself on being a school dedicated to the development of the autonomy of the individual. This stance continues to resist the rather neutral phrase "architectural education."

In perusing the set of drawings, one might the ask question – why is there a clear preference for all things Italian? Might the answer be in the astounding density of visual culture, in particular, of Ancient, Medieval, and Renaissance Italian architecture? Here a vernacular hill-town is equal to the work of a known master. Clarity of authorship is not required for this "structuralist" and anti-historical attitude toward situating the drawings. The place-to-place density of Italy offers a "movable feast." Egger's drawn pedagogy has an especially deep affinity with and respect for Rome – a city comprised of layers the act of drawing peels away at will.

Professor Egger is immersed and encompassed within the places and buildings he draws. Using techniques of modernity, he pulls and dematerializes historical places forward in time like Gideon's "eternal present." He renders the opacity of stone and stucco as transparent and crystalline as if the world is made of lines. Spaces wrap around and surround him as he draws them. This sense of being spatially surrounded is the same feeling one has when viewing the drawings as well. A viewer is projected behind the drawn space in front of them in a modern reversal of the frontal nature of the drawing surface. The flat Renaissance picture plane elliptically warps to make spaces that literally and phenomenally surround the viewer as perspectival forms of quasi-mathematical spatial becoming. Even the floors of piazzas seem transparent as if we can see through them like a horizontal window; drawn as if they are traces of an unseen and yet to be revealed topography and topology. In the examples showcased in this publication, there is a precise willing and volition depicting the world as designs emerging from the interrelations of lines. This is an adventurous science of lines modified by an active willing. If according to Hannah Arendt we can credit St. Augustine with the birth of the modern idea of the human will, how can we bring that willing into the education of an architect? Here the sheer discipline and density of Egger's lines curb any possible excess leaning towards mere willfulness. The will of an architect is clearly expressed in these disciplined and carefully delineated sketches.

The sketches simultaneously employ the techniques and devices of perspective and cubism with origins in the art of painting. They employ multiple points of views and horizons. There is a fusion of horizon lines and vanishing points allowing the eye of the viewer to travel within the drawing. In this sense, they are combinatory of both Renaissance virtue and Modern virtue. They often seek and are in search of the virtue of a place or building. The selection of places visited and drawn in-situ serves as a check and filter to unfettered experience becoming an avenue to virtue. Virtue becomes the basis of choice and judgment undergirding design. What one selects as a subject of interest is as important as how one sketches that subject. Importantly there is a moral foundation to the scenographic aspect of the sketches often left out in most contemporary, virtual reality-based visualizations. Egger's sketches bring virtue to reality. This visual morality makes them much more meaningful than typical and perhaps more charming travel sketches. Students traveling with Professor Egger seek their own sense of morality relative to what they see. Sketching in this sense becomes central to the moral education of an architect's eye.

A FACULTY IN ARCHITECTURE IS ONLY AS GOOD AS THE BOOKS THEY HAVE READ to assist them in distilling the visceral experience of travel. Egger's library is the storeroom and ballast for his teaching architecture through sketching. Volumes by Ivan Illich, Jerome Brunner, Rudolph Arnheim, Henri Bergson sit on the shelves. Alfred North Whitehead's "process philosophy" articulated in his book *Process and Reality* along with *Adventures in Ideas* are critical sources of epistemic influence upon his pedagogy. His sketches are visual and spatial understandings of these important thinkers. From Whitehead emerges a new philosophy of the primacy of the processual and the relational imbued with an overall sense of adventure. The decidedly modern philosophy of becoming challenges ancient notions of fixity, stasis and being.

THE PEDAGOGY OF THE SKETCH

Egger's sketches are in search of an active and entangled science of the visual available for students of architecture – enabling them to become architects one day.

Given the long arc of the many decades that have passed during the period of Professor Egger's involvement traveling and sketching with students, one can sense the flavor of each decade in each line of every drawing. The ink never ossifies into an ontological absolute. Instead, the conscious and elegant refusal of ontology, at the heart of his pedagogical philosophy, is in some way a remarkable form of lived ontology and a permanent contribution to the education of generations of architects and their teachers.

Postscript: There is one sketch that Professor Egger has drawn showing the front elevation of the Temple of Minerva in Assisi, Italy that is of particular importance. It was my privilege to be present while this drawing was made in-situ. For economy, it shows half of a symmetrical façade with a vertical centerline indicated. Like many of the other sketches, Egger draws on Italian-made Fabriano paper embossed with the famous logo on the bottom left of the sheet. The drawing is of the same Roman temple Goethe wrote about so poetically in his *Italian Journey*. This elevation study stands as an exception in the overall set of travel sketches as it brackets out both perspective and its related horizon. The order of the temple front is made intelligible through number, proportion, symmetry, and geometry showing 'true' heights and widths. The drawing has a stunning and meticulous elegance capturing in great detail a single Corinthian column capital within its intelligible web. On careful inspection, one can read the fine curvature of the entasis of the column as the curved lines of the flutes come imperceptibly closer at the top of the shaft. There are other areas of the half elevation demarcated in selected detail at the base, the left edge of the facade and pediment of the temple. Unlike Palladio's drawing of the same temple Egger's shows the slope of the grade at the base of the building. The actuality of this line is remarkable at it meets the ideal order of the temple. The drawing in effect constructs the paradox of the temple in its primary ideality grounded in the particularity of a place. It is a drawing by an architect for other architects. One has the sense this is the phenomenon of architecture standing before the eyes and mind of an architect.

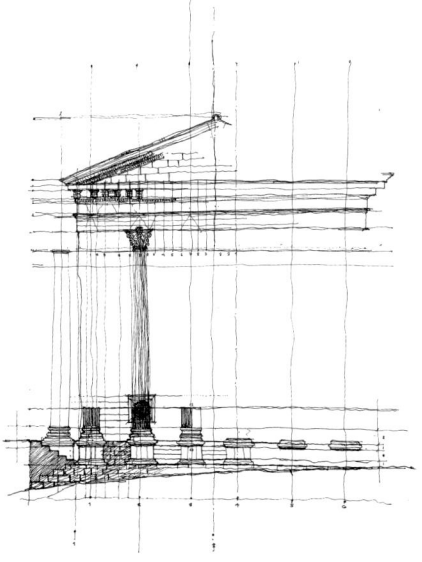

TEMPLE OF MINERVA - PIAZZA DEL COMMUNE
Italy, Assisi (October 1994)
Pen and Ink Drawing on Fabriano Paper
33.02 cm x 48.26 cm (13 in x 19 in)

ARCO DEI BECCI E CUGNANESI
Italy, San Gimignano (13 November 1990)
Pen and Ink Drawing on Fabriano Paper
33.02 cm x 48.26 cm (13 in x 19 in)

Biographies

CONTRIBUTORS

RICHARD BLYTHE, PH.D. | Richard Blythe is the Dean of the College of Architecture and Urban Studies (CAUS) at Virginia Tech. Dr. Blythe previously served as the Dean of the School of Architecture + Design at RMIT University (Australia), as a Visiting Research Professor at Queen's University, Belfast, and in 2010, he established the RMIT Practice-based Research Ph.D. program in Europe and Asia. He is a recipient of the prestigious Velux Professorial fellowship, Aarhus School of Architecture in Denmark and the founding director of the architecture practice Terroir and Company where he served as Director until 2012. He continues to contribute to the Terroir team. Richard currently serves as an Advisory Board Member for the Ashgate Publishing's Design Research in Architecture Series and a review editor for Routledge and the European online journal *JAR*.

KENNETH FRAMPTON | Professor Kenneth Frampton is an architect, architectural historian, and critic of contemporary and modern architecture. Professor Frampton studied architecture at Guildford School of Art and the Architectural Association School of Architecture, London. He is a professor of history and theory of architecture at Columbia University. He has been a member of the faculty at Columbia University since 1972, and that same year he became a fellow of the Institute for Architecture and Urban Studies in New York and a co-founding editor of its magazine *Oppositions*. His numerous publications include *Modern Architecture and the Critical Present* (1980), *Studies in Tectonic Culture* (1995), *American Masterworks* (1995), *Le Corbusier* (2001), *Labour, Work & Architecture* (2005), and an updated fourth edition of *Modern Architecture: A Critical History* (2007).

DAYTON EUGENE EGGER | Dayton Eugene Egger is the Patrick and Nancy Lathrop Professor Emeritus, Virginia Tech School of Architecture + Design. A member of the Virginia Tech community since 1969, Egger has contributed significantly to the teaching mission of the architecture studio at the Center for European Studies and Architecture in Riva San Vitale, Switzerland. He also aided in the advancement of the international education abroad program as director of special programs for the College of Architecture and Urban Studies. Egger was awarded the Alumni Award for Excellence in International Programs and named the international president of the Phi Beta Delta honor society for international scholars. In the classroom, Egger taught a wide range of architecture courses to both undergraduate and graduate students. He served as chair of the Academy of Teaching Excellence, as the assistant dean for undergraduate studies, the chair of the foundation program, and the director of the industrial design program. Egger received the William E. Wine Award and has participated extensively in university governance by serving as chair of the William E. Wine Award Committee and the Commission on International Affairs and Outreach. Egger received his Bachelor of Architecture degree from Auburn University and a master's degree from Virginia Tech.

STEVEN + CATHI HOUSE | Since 1982 House + House Architects have crafted intimate, personal architecture, producing a diverse body of work reflecting their passion for site-specific, well-choreographed buildings in California, Mexico, and the Caribbean. In their humane and handcrafted modernism, Cathi and Steven think with infused spatial color, inclusive boundaries, and sculpted natural light, resulting in environments where the passage is as relevant as the arrival. Their work demonstrates a commitment to sustainability and green building and focuses on enduring design principles incorporating natural light and ventilation, passive solar heating, grey/rainwater systems, recycled materials, and the development of micro-climates with strong connections between indoor and outdoor spaces. House + House has received more than 50 design awards, and numerous national and international publications featured their work. Cathi and Steven have lectured extensively throughout the United States and Mexico and have both served on the Dean's Advisory Board for the College of Architecture and Urban Studies at Virginia Tech. They have established CASA, The Center for Architecture, Sustainability + Art, a new architecture study abroad program based in San Miguel de Allende, Mexico, recently designated a UNESCO World Heritage Site.

MITZI VERNON | Mitzi Vernon is the Dean of the College of Design at the University of Kentucky. Most recently, she was Professor of Industrial Design in the School of Architecture + Design at Virginia Tech. Her career spans 30 years of leadership, practice, and teaching in industrial design, engineering, and architecture. As the originator of the project, Fields Everywhere, she has been a recipient of several patents and grants supporting her research in using design to teach science to children. She was one of the inaugural speakers for TEDx Virginia Tech, delivering Mapping the Invisible in 2012. She is an Edward Singleton Diggs Teaching Scholar, and among other awards, Virginia Tech honored her with a 2008 Dell ReGeneration International Design Educator Award and the prestigious William E. Wine Award for Excellence in Teaching. An emerging stream of her research is the pedagogy of product form.

PAUL EMMONS, PH.D. | Paul Emmons is an architect and professor at the Washington Alexandria Architecture Center of Virginia Tech, where he coordinates the Ph.D. program in Architecture + Design Research. He is also Associate Dean of Graduate Studies for the College of Architecture and Urban Studies. Dr. Emmons earned a Master of Architecture from the University of Minnesota and a Ph.D. from the University of Pennsylvania. His research has been presented around the world, focusing on theories of practice and drawing in architectural design. In addition to his forthcoming book *Drawing Imagining Building: Embodiment in Architectural Drawing Practices*; he is co-editor of *Confabulations, Storytelling in Architecture* (2017) and *The Cultural Role of Architecture* (2012).

MARK BLIZARD | Mark Blizard is an associate professor and former department chair in the College of Architecture, Construction, and Planning at the University of Texas at San Antonio where he has taught since 1998. Blizard holds his architectural registration in the state of Maryland and before coming to San Antonio, has practiced in Washington D.C., Blacksburg, Virginia, and Charlotte, North Carolina. He received both his Bachelor of Architecture and Masters of Architecture at Virginia Tech (1986 and 1988), where he taught for six years from 1992 to 1998. In 2008, Professor Blizard published his first book of architectural theory and practice titled, *Architecture: Land Culture Practic*e. He is also the author of the upcoming book, *Meditations on the Sketch: An Architect Travels in Italy* and has written numerous papers on subjects relating to landscape and memory, urban form, and practice as bricolage. Since 2009, Blizard has developed, directed and taught in the UTSA's study abroad program in Castiglion Fiorentino and Urbino, Italy.

MICHAEL OBRIEN | Michael OBrien is an architect and professor of architecture at Texas A&M University. He served as a guest curator for the National Building Museum, an on-screen expert for the Discovery Channel, and former president of the Architectural Research Centers Consortium. His research focuses on the topic of housing, the historical development of the light-wood frame in America, the design of affordable, modular and mobile-home based housing. The U.S. Department of Housing and Urban Development published his scholarship on information flows and industrialized control methods for contemporary housing. Professor OBrien has also conducted extensive studies on the interaction of formal and informal spatial structures in the subdivisions and new towns of John Nolen, and of the structural types in Louis Sullivan's architectural ornament. He teaches undergraduate and graduate design studios and lectures on the interrelationships between architectural ideas and construction. He holds degrees in architecture from North Dakota State University and Virginia Tech.

GREGORY LUHAN, PH.D. | Dr. Gregory Luhan, is the John Russell Groves Endowed Professor of Architecture in the UK College of Design and an affiliate professor with UK's Lewis Honors College and the College of Engineering Center for Visualization and Virtual Environments. Luhan holds a University Research Professorship and is a nationally recognized architect, scholar, author, professor and academic leader whose work investigates how design, emerging digital technologies, critical theory, pedagogy, practice and academic-industry partnerships intersect. He earned his Bachelor of Architecture from Virginia Tech, Master of Architecture from Princeton University, and doctorate at Texas A&M University. Dr. Luhan teaches Architecture and Historic Preservation digital studios and seminars on design theory, systems thinking and design computing. Dr. Luhan's professional practice includes award-winning, research-driven projects which enabled him to forge collaborative relationships with disciplines outside architecture, most notably engineering, education, business, physics, arts & sciences, and the fine arts.

FRANK H. WEINER | Professor Weiner has been a faculty member in Virginia Tech's School of Architecture + Design since 1987 teaching design studios and seminars. He has widely published his scholarship on the intersections of architecture, the education of an architect and philosophy. He has presented papers at academic venues in China, Denmark, Finland, Germany, Israel, Japan, United Kingdom, Russia and the USA. He has served in a variety of administrative positions in the School of Architecture + Design including the Head of the Department of Architecture (1997-2003) and the Founding Interim Director of the School (2003). He has served as a visiting critic at Pratt Institute, Penn State, Clemson University, and the University of Virginia. He is the recipient of the 2003-2005 EAAE prize. In addition to his teaching duties, he serves as the founding curator of the Lucy and Olivio Ferrari Archive established in 2017 at Virginia Tech. He is a graduate of Tulane University (1980), Columbia University (1987) and is a registered architect in the State of New York.